How to knit
BEAUTIFUL
BAGS

Dedication

To my daughters, Hannah and Rhiannon, and to my partner, David, for their ongoing interest and encouragement, and for not complaining about the house filling up with endless amounts of yarn.

How to Knit
BEAUTIFUL
BAGS
22 gorgeous designs

Sian Brown

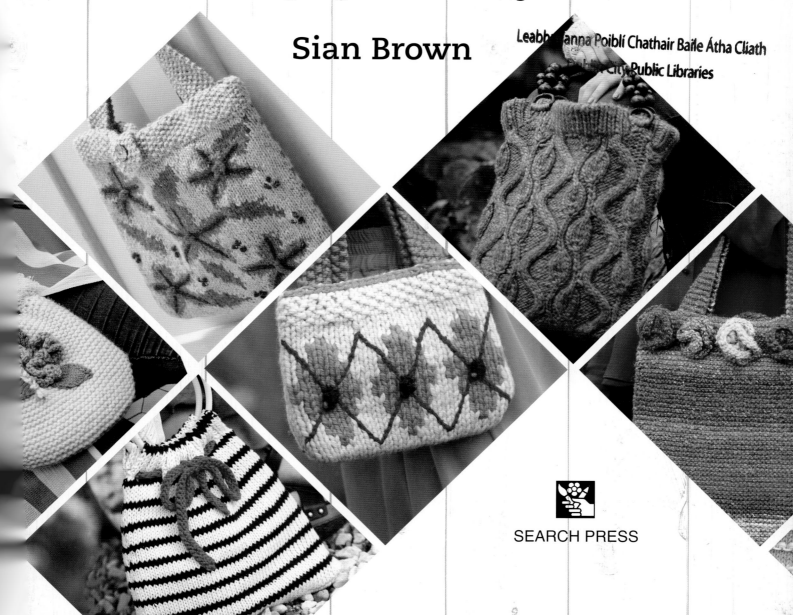

SEARCH PRESS

Acknowledgements

A big thank you to the following at Search Press: to Katie French for coming up with the idea for the book and for commissioning it; to May Corfield and Becky Robbins for their editing skills.
Thanks also to the yarn companies who kindly provided the yarn: Designer Yarns, Rowan, Rico, Sirdar, Sublime, Artesano, and Wool Warehouse for the Drops yarn; to the fabric companies Ditto Fabrics and myfabrics.co.uk for providing some of the fabrics; and to my pattern writer, Bronagh Miskelly, and my team of knitters for their hard work.

First published in 2018

Search Press Limited
Wellwood, North Farm Road,
Tunbridge Wells, Kent TN2 3DR

Photographs by Roddy Paine Studios

Additional photographs by Paul Bricknell at Search Press studios: 4, 11, 13, 19, 23t, 26, 31t, 35t, 39t, 43b, 46t, 47, 51, 55, 59t, 63t, 67b, 71b, 75b, 78b, 82b, 87t, 90b, 94b, 98b, 102b, 112t, 117, 120.

Text copyright © Sian Brown 2018

Photographs and design copyright
© Search Press Ltd 2018

ISBN: 978-1-78221-308-6

The Publishers and author can accept no responsibility for any consequences arising from the information, advice or instructions given in this publication.

Suppliers
For details of suppliers, please visit the Search Press website: www.searchpress.com

Printed in China by 1010 Printing International Ltd

CONTENTS

Simple Bags

Summer Bags

44 48

52 56

60 64

68 72

Cablework

Evening

76   80

84

88   92

96   100

Colourwork

INTRODUCTION

I have always loved having a choice of bags that I can change throughout the year, depending on the season and my wardrobe. I spend a lot of my time designing garments and home knits, and being asked to do a book of knitted bags was an interesting and refreshingly different design project. Bags are relatively quick to make, and can allow you to try some new techniques. Creative inspiration has come from all kinds of bags, and from the yarns, stitches and colours chosen for the designs. I have put together a group of designs that range from simple projects for beginners, to more advanced cable and colourwork bags, in sizes from small and delicate to larger everyday practical bags.

The yarns used are varied and include pure wools, wool mixes, alpaca and alpaca mixes, cotton and silk. All of the bags are lined and have pockets, and most have wadding/batting to make the bags firmer and more practical. The book is divided into sections: Simple Bags, Summer Bags, Evening, Cablework and Colourwork.

The Simple Bags are worked in basic stitches and knit and purl textures – some with simple knitted flowers – and are good for beginners. The Summer Bags are in cotton yarns and include textured stitches, knitted flowers, appliqué and embroidery. The Evening bags are worked in delicate lace stitches, or intarsia with embroidery and sequins. The Cablework bags have a variety of cables for more advanced knitters. In Colourwork, the bags use all-over Fair Isle and a Fair Isle border with rib and intarsia.

I have included generic yarns in the patterns themselves – as long as you use the same weight and approximate yardage, you should have enough yarn to make the bags. If you want details of the actual yarns used for the bags, see the list on page 127.

These patterns will enable you to create individual, distinctive bags that can be used for a range of different looks and occasions. I have really enjoyed working on this book, and I hope it will inspire you to make a few beautiful knitted bags of your own.

Sian

Knitting is a simple craft that requires few tools and materials. If you are a keen knitter, you will already have a selection of knitting needles and even various yarns left over from other projects. That's really all you need to get started. Most people have scissors and measuring tools; on these pages, there are some suggestions for other items you will find useful.

Yarn

There is a huge variety of yarn available, from natural animal and plant fibres to man made or mixes. The yarns used in this book include pure wool, wool mixes, wool/alpaca, fine kid mohair silk mix, cotton, silk, alpaca mix and eyelash yarn. The yarn for each project is carefully chosen for its qualities to work with the shape, stitch and design.

Other yarns can be substituted, if they use the same needle size and tension (gauge), and the bag will look better if a similar type of yarn is used. The yarn band carries useful information such as the suggested needle size and tension (gauge), the fibre content and wash care instructions.

Knitting needles

There are three basic types of knitting needles: straight needles, circular needles and double-pointed needles (DPN). A cable needle is a shorter version of a DPN, used to hold a small number of stitches while working on a cable pattern.

Knitting needles tend to be mainly made from metal, wood such as bamboo or rosewood and plastic. It is a matter of personal preference what you choose. Experiment to find which kind suits you best.

Sewing machine

A basic model of sewing machine is all you need to stitch together the bag linings with the wadding/batting and the pockets and interfacing to the lining.

Scissors

A small pair of scissors is an essential part of your knitting kit. It is always best to cut yarn and not break it. Fabric scissors are also used in this book to cut lining fabric, wadding/batting and interfacing.

Tape measure

A tape measure is another useful part of your knitting kit. It is used to measure a tension (gauge) swatch, which is always worth doing before starting a project, and to check throughout knitting to make sure that the measurements are accurate. The lining fabrics need to be measured before cutting. A ruler can also be used to check tension (gauge).

Pins

These are used to pin knitted or fabric pieces together before sewing them up. They are also used to mark lining fabric before cutting, and for pinning out knitted pieces before blocking them (see page 115).

Bobbins

Bobbins are used when knitting an intarsia pattern. Small amounts of each colour can be wound onto them to help prevent the yarn from becoming tangled.

Tapestry needle

This is a chunky needle with a large eye and a blunt end used with yarn to sew knitted pieces together, and also for embroidery. A smaller sewing needle (with a pointed end) is used to hand sew fabric and to sew on buttons, beads and sequins.

Sewing thread

This is used to machine sew the linings, and to hand sew the linings to the bags. It is also used to sew on buttons, beads, snap fasteners and braided handles. A small sewing needle is used for this thread.

Bought handles

There are a good variety of bought handles available. The ones used in this book include plastic circular, faux leather plain with tabs, faux leather plaited, beaded, bamboo and wooden. They introduce some variety into the way the bags are finished.

Magnetic closures

These are a useful way of fastening the sides of a bag together. They are neat, easy to use and do not show on the outside of the bags.

Snap fasteners

These are used with button tabs to make the bag easier and quicker to open and close.

Buttons

These are used as decorations on tabs that have snap fasteners underneath as the main bag closure.

Wadding/batting

Wadding/batting is a bulky material used to make the bags firmer, unless very chunky yarn is used or the bags are light and delicate. The most popular weight is 135g (4oz) per square metre, which I have used for the projects here.

Interfacing

This is used on the pockets for all of the bags to make them nice and firm. The iron-on type is quick and easy to use.

Beads and sequins

These are attached to the finished bags to add interest to some of the designs. They are attached with sewing thread. They can also be knitted in as you work, but the ones used here are added after making up the bags.

Ribbon

This can be used to make ties for a lacy style of bag. It gives projects a delicate look.

Faux suede cord

This cord is soft and flexible and can easily be made into a braid to form a bag tie. The texture contrasts well with yarn. The type I have used is 3mm (1/8in) wide.

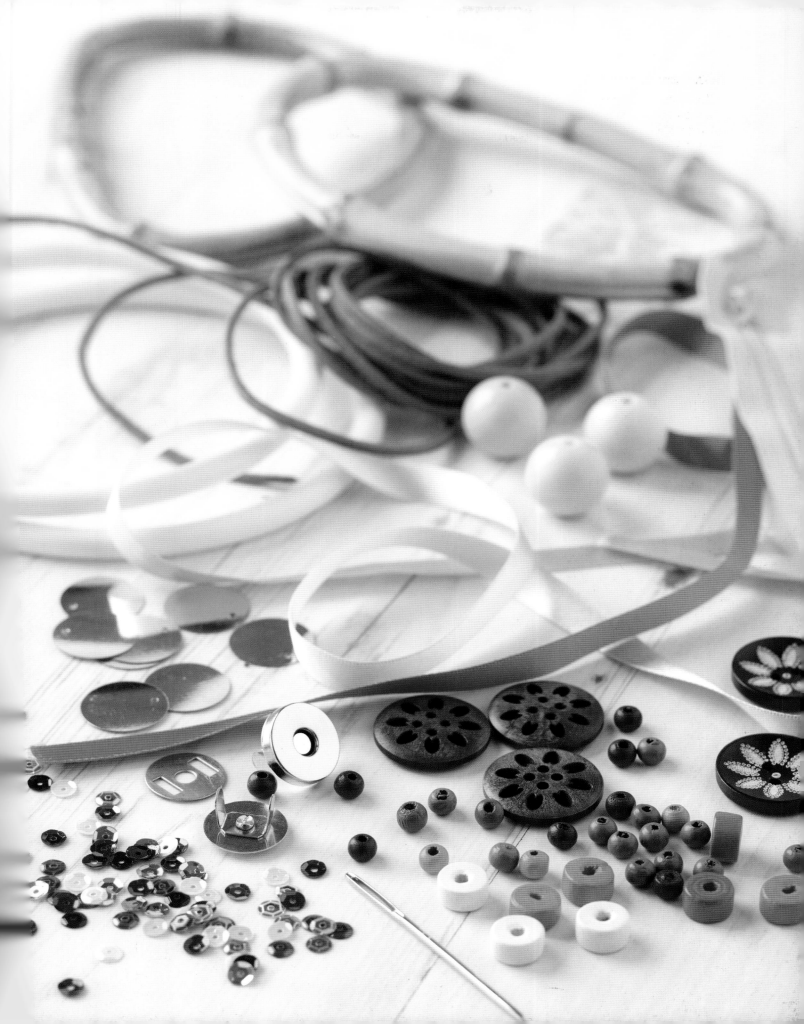

The

Bags

Simple Bags

FLOWERS & BEADS

 *Beginner*

This pretty little bag is quick and easy to make. Worked in garter stitch, it includes a pretty beaded handle in matching candy colours, a braided yarn drawstring and appliquéd leaves with knitted flowers.

INSTRUCTIONS

FRONT AND BACK (MAKE 2)

Using yarn A and 6mm (UK 4, US 10) needles, cast on 26 sts.
Working in g st (k every row) throughout, increase work as follows.
Row 1: knit.
Row 2: k1, m1, k to end (27 sts).
Row 3: k1, m1, k to end (28 sts).
Continue to increase in this way to row 15 (40 sts).
Continue in g st until work measures 22cm (8½in) from cast-on edge.
Eyelet row: k4, (k2tog, yo, k3) six times, k2tog, yf, k4.
Work 2 rows g st.
Change to yarn B.
Work 5 rows g st.
Cast off.

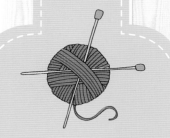

Equipment

KNITTING NEEDLES

6mm (UK 4, US 10)
4.5mm (UK 7, US 7)

MATERIALS

2 balls of chunky (bulky) yarn in cream (A); 100g/110m/120yd

1 ball of chunky (bulky) fur-style yarn in cream (B); 50g/60m/65yd

1 ball of aran (10-ply/worsted) yarn in mauve (C) and green (D); 50g/90m/98yd

16 15mm (½in) beads

17 spacer beads

Picture wire, or thin covered wire

Magnetic closure

Lining and wadding/batting: 27 x 51cm (10¾ x 20in)

Lining for pocket: 15 x 33cm (6 x 13in)

Interfacing for pocket: 12 x 12cm (4¾ x 4¾in)

TENSION (GAUGE)

14 sts x 29 rows over 10 x 10cm (4 x 4in) in g st using 6mm (UK 4, US 10) needles

FINISHED SIZE

24 x 24cm (9½ x 9½in) excluding handle

FLOWERS (MAKE 3)

Using yarn C and 4.5mm (UK 7, US 7) needles, cast on 49 sts.

Row 1: knit.

Row 2: purl.

Row 3: k1, *k2, pass first st over second st, rep from * to end (25 sts).

Row 4: (p2tog) twelve times, p1 (13 sts).

Row 5: k1 (k2tog) six times (7 sts).

Pull yarn through remaining sts, leaving a length to sew onto bag.

LEAVES (MAKE 3)

Using yarn D and 4.5mm (UK 7, US 7) needles, cast on 3 sts.

Row 1: knit.

Row 2: purl.

Row 3: k1, M1, k1, M1, k1 (5 sts).

Row 4 (and every other row): purl.

Row 5: k1, M1, k3, M1 (7 sts).

Row 7: k1, M1, k5, M1, k1 (9 sts).

Work 7 rows in st st.

Row 15: k2tog, k to last 2 sts, k2tog (7 sts).

Row 17: k2tog, k to last 2 sts, k2tog (5 sts).

Row 19: k2tog, k1, k2tog (3 sts).

Next row: p2tog, p1.

Next row: k2tog.

Cast off.

TIE

Cut six strands of yarns A and C, all 90cm (35½in) long. Separate into three lots of two strands and braid them to form a tie. Make a knot in each end.

HANDLE

To make the handle, cut three 50cm (19¾in) lengths of wire and twist them together. Thread large beads and spacers between, starting and ending with a spacer bead. Pull tightly and make the ends into loops.

APPLIQUÉ AND FLOWERS

Pin the leaves to the bag using the photographs for guidance, with cast-on edges pointing to the centre. Sew them in place using yarn D. Arrange and secure the flowers to the centre, using lengths from the cast-off row.

MAKING UP

Mark the lining fabric around the shape of the knitted pieces, following the curve at the bottom.

Leave a seam allowance of 1.5cm (⅝in), cut out the lining and set aside.

Cut two small squares from the remaining lining fabric, and turn over the ends. Pin them around the loops of wire to cover them and hand sew in place, securing well at the top. Pin the bottom of the bag right sides together and sew the seam using backstitch (see page 116). Then sew the side seams using mattress stitch (see page 117).

Now make the lining, following the instructions on page 122, and the magnetic closure instructions on page 121. Pin the lining in place, just below the eyelets, inserting the handle wire loops under the fabric at the sides. Slip stitch the lining in place, securing it around the handles. If there is any wire showing above the lining, sew some yarn around it to cover it. Thread the tie through the eyelets.

Simple Bags

FLOWER BASKET

 Beginner

With simple garter stitch handles and top, this design features an attractive, basket-weave pattern for the body of the bag. Topped off with a delicate flower in a complementary colour using lightweight, mohair yarn, add some matching seed beads for a bit of sparkle and shine.

INSTRUCTIONS

FRONT AND BACK (MAKE 2)
With yarn A, cast on 63 sts.
Row 1: knit.
Row 2: purl.
Row 3 (RS): k4, *p7, k5, rep from * to last 11 sts, p7, k4.
Row 4: p4, *k7, p5, rep from * to last 11 sts, k7, p4.
Row 5: knit.
Row 6: purl.
Row 7: as row 3.
Row 8: as row 4.
Row 9: knit.
Row 10: purl.
Row 11: p5, *k5, p7, rep from * to last 10 sts, k5, p5.
Row 12: k5, *p5, k7, rep from * to last 10 sts, p5, k5.
Row 13: knit.
Row 14: purl.
Row 15: as row 11.
Row 16: as row 12.
These 16 rows form the pattern. Repeat three more times, then work rows 1–8 once more.
Work 30 rows knit.
Cast off.

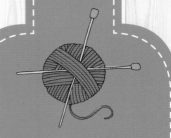

Equipment

KNITTING NEEDLES
4.5mm (UK 7, US 7)

MATERIALS
4 balls of aran (10-ply/worsted) yarn in mauve (A); 50g/98yd/90m
Small amount of 1–3-ply (lace weight) yarn in lilac (B); 25g/218yd/200m
16 lilac seed beads
Magnetic closure
Lining and wadding/batting: 36 x 29cm (14 x 11½in)
Lining for pocket: 18 x 33cm (7 x 13in)
Interfacing for pocket: 15 x 15cm (6 x 6in)

TENSION (GAUGE)
24 sts x 32 rows over 10 x 10cm (4 x 4in) in pattern

FINISHED SIZE
33 x 26cm (13 x 10¼in) excluding handles

HANDLE (MAKE 2)

With yarn A, cast on 8 sts. Knit until handle measures 40cm (15¾in).
Cast off.

FLOWER (MAKE 5 PETALS)

Using yarn B held double, cast on 6 sts.
Row 1: knit.
Row 2: purl.
Repeat these 2 rows three more times.
Row 9: k2tog, k2, k2tog (4 sts).
Row 10: purl.
Row 11: k2tog twice (2 sts).
Row 12: purl.
Row 13: k2tog.
Fasten off.

MAKING UP

Press the main pieces of the bag under a damp cloth (see page 115 for Blocking). Pin the flower petals to one side of the bag with the cast-on edges at the centre and sew in place. Sew the beads in the centre of the flower.

With right sides facing, pin and sew the bottom seam using backstitch (see page 116). Then sew the side seams using mattress stitch (see page 117). Turn over the top border to half the depth, and slip stitch it in place. Pin and sew the handles to the inside top of the bag.

Follow the lining instructions on page 122 to make and fit the lining and pocket, and the instructions on page 121 to fit the magnetic closure.

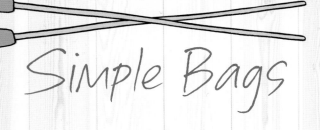

Simple Bags

TEXTURED CIRCLES

 Beginner/Intermediate

This stylish bag features faux leather handles and a suede cord drawstring to set off the lovely textured surface and provide a pop of colour.

INSTRUCTIONS

FRONT AND BACK (MAKE 2)
Cast on 69 sts.
Row 1: purl.
Start pattern:
Work 3 rows reversed st st, starting with a k row (WS).
Row 5: k7, sl 5, *k5, sl 5, rep from * to last 7 sts, k7.
Row 6: p7, sl 5, *p5, sl 5, rep from * to last 7 sts, p7.
Rep last 2 rows once more then row 5 again.
Work 3 rows reversed st st, starting with a k row.
Row 13: k2, sl 5, *k5, sl 5, rep from * to last 2 sts, k2.
Row 14: p2, sl 5, *p5, sl 5, rep from * to last 2 sts, p2.
Rep the last 2 rows once more, then row 13 again.
These 16 rows form the pattern.
Work 6 whole repeats, then rows 2–9 once more.
Eyelet row: k8, (k2tog, yf, k8) five times, k2tog, yf, k9.
Work 12 rows g st.
Cast off.

Equipment

KNITTING NEEDLES
4.5mm (UK 7, US 7)

MATERIALS
3 balls of aran (10-ply/worsted) yarn in grey; 50g/88m/96yd

Handles: faux leather cream 32cm (12½in) long, not including tabs

Faux suede cord: 3mm x 3m (⅛ x 118½in)

Lining and wadding/batting: 35 x 55cm (13¾ x 21¾in)

Lining for pocket: 17 x 34cm (6½ x 13½in)

Interfacing for pocket: 14 x 14cm (5½ x 5½in)

TENSION (GAUGE)
20 sts x 42 rows over 10 x 10cm (4 x 4in) in pattern

FINISHED SIZE
32 x 26cm (12½ x 10¼in) excluding handles

MAKING UP

Block and press the edges of the bag under a damp cloth
(see page 115). Pin the bottom of the bag right sides
together and sew the seam using backstitch (see page
116). Then sew the side seams using mattress stitch
(see page 117).

To make and attach the lining, follow the instructions on
page 122. Make sure that you sew the lining just below the
level of the eyelets.

TIE

Cut the faux suede cord into three pieces and braid them to form a tie. Thread the braid through the eyelets and tie in a bow at the front of the bag. Attach the handles to the bag following the maker's instructions.

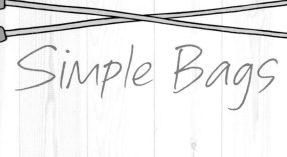

Simple Bags

ROSES

 Beginner

Worked in a beautiful, soft aran (10-ply/worsted) yarn, this bag is deceptively easy to make. A simple garter stitch in this multicoloured yarn looks very striking and the roses set it off perfectly.

INSTRUCTIONS

FRONT AND BACK (MAKE 2)
Cast on 60 sts.
Work in g st (k every row) until work measures 30cm (11¾in).
Cast off.

HANDLE (MAKE 2)
Cast on 10 sts.
Work in g st until handle measures 40cm (15¾in).
Cast off.

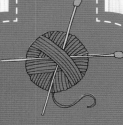

Equipment

KNITTING NEEDLES

4.5mm (UK 7, US 7)

MATERIALS

4 balls of aran (10-ply/
worsted) yarn in purple/
orange/green multicoloured;
50g/100m/110yd
Lining and wadding/batting:
34 x 60cm (13½ x 23¾in)
Lining for pocket:
18 x 33cm (7 x 13in)
Interfacing for pocket:
15 x 15 cm (6 x 6in)

TENSION (GAUGE)

19 sts x 35 rows over
10 x 10cm (4 x 4in) in g st

FINISHED SIZE

31 x 30cm (12 x 11¾in)
excluding handles

ROSES (MAKE 10)

Cast on 49 sts.

Row 1: knit.

Row 2: purl.

Row 3: k1, *k2, pass first st over second st; rep from * to end (25 sts).

Row 4: *p2tog, rep from * to last st, p1 (13 sts).

Row 5: k1, (k2tog) six times (7 sts).

Thread yarn through remaining sts.

Fasten off.

MAKING UP

Block and press the front and back pieces under a damp cloth (see page 115).

Pin the bottom of the bag right sides together and sew the seam using backstitch (see page 116). Then sew the side seams using mattress stitch (see page 117). Fold over 3cm (1¼in) at the top, pin and slip stitch in place. Pin the handles to start where the top has been folded over, and sew in place. Pin and sew the flowers across the top (see page 113), placing five flowers on each side.

To make and attach the lining, follow the instructions on page 122.

TWO-TONE

 *Beginner*

The pretty two-tone effect in this bag is made by holding strands of two different colours together. The look is completed with a braided drawstring and pompoms. There is also a co-ordinating make-up bag or coin purse to make if you wish.

INSTRUCTIONS

FRONT AND BACK (MAKE 2)
Using one strand of A and B together throughout, cast on 35 sts.
Work in g st (k every row) until work measures 25cm (10in).
Eyelet row: k4, (k2tog, yf, k4) four times, k2tog, yf, k5.
Work g st for another 4cm (1½in).
Cast off.

HANDLE (MAKE 2)
Cast on 6 sts.
Work in g st until handle measures 40cm (15¾in).
Cast off.

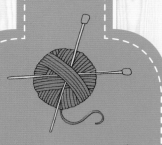

Equipment

KNITTING NEEDLES
6.5mm (UK 3, US 10½)

MATERIALS
(NB: the yarn amounts will make the bag and purse)
2 balls of aran (10-ply/worsted) yarn in cream (A); 100g/200m/220yd
3 balls of aran (10-ply/worsted) yarn in yellow (B); 50g/87m/95yd
15cm (6in) zip for purse
Lining and wadding/batting for bag: 28 x 60cm (11 x 23¼in)
Lining for pocket: 18 x 33cm (7 x 13in)
Interfacing for pocket: 15 x 15cm (6 x 6in)
Lining for purse: 18 x 23cm (7 x 9in)
Interfacing for purse: 18 x 23cm (7 x 9in)

TENSION (GAUGE)
14 sts x 26 rows over 10 x 10cm (4 x 4in) in g st, using yarns A and B together

FINISHED SIZE
Bag: 25 x 30cm (9¾ x 11¾in) excluding handles
Coin purse/make-up bag: 16 x 10cm (6¼ x 4in)

TIE

Cut six strands of either colour or a mix of both, all 75cm (29½in) long. Braid to form a tie. Make two pompoms (see page 114) and trim to size in either colour or a mix of both. Leave some of the strands long.

MAKING UP

Block and press pieces under a damp cloth (see page 115). Pin the bottom of the bag right sides together and sew the seam using backstitch (see page 116). Then sew the side seams using mattress stitch (see page 117). Pin the handles in place and sew. Sew one pompom onto the end of the tie. Thread the other end of the tie through the eyelets. Sew the second pompom onto the other end of the tie.

To make and attach the lining, follow the instructions on page 122. Ensure that you attach the lining just under the eyelets.

COIN PURSE OR MAKE–UP BAG

Cast on 25 sts.
Work in g st (k every row) until work measures 20cm (8in).
Cast off.

MAKING UP

Block and press the purse pieces under a damp cloth (see page 115). Sew the side seams together using mattress stitch (see page 117). To attach the zip and lining, follow the instructions on pages 118 and 122.

Simple Bags

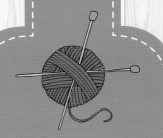

FOLK

 Beginner

This sweet little shoulder bag has a fun, braided fabric strap and small flowers embroidered onto the front and back. Make sure you do the embroidery before making up the bag, as it will be much easier. The blanket stitch edging accents the front flap and the pocket, and there's a coin purse to match.

INSTRUCTIONS

BAG (MAKE IN 1 PIECE)
Using yarn A, cast on 34 sts.
Row 1: *k1, p1; rep from * to end.
Row 2: *p1, k1; rep from * to end.
These 2 rows form moss st.
Repeat these 2 rows until work measures 40cm (15¾in).
Continue in moss st as set, cast off 9 sts at the beginning of the next 2 rows (16 sts).
Continue in moss st for another 6cm (2½in).
Cast off.

KNITTED POCKET
Using yarn A, cast on 16 sts.
Row 1: *k1, p1; rep from * to end.
Row 2: *p1, k1; rep from * to end.
Repeat these 2 rows until pocket measures 7cm (2¾in).
Cast off.

Equipment

KNITTING NEEDLES
4.5mm (UK 7, US 7)

MATERIALS
(NB: the yarn amounts will make the bag and purse)
2 balls of aran (10-ply/worsted) yarn in dark red (A); 50g/70m/76yd
Small amounts of aran (10-ply/worsted) yarn in green (B), blue (C), pink (D), orange (E), white (F) and yellow (G); 50g/75m/82yd
2 15mm (½in) buttons
2 snap fasteners
10cm (4in) zip for purse
Lining and wadding/batting: 25 x 54cm (9¾ x 21¼in)
Lining for pocket:15 x 27cm (6 x 10⅝in)
Interfacing for pocket: 12 x 12cm (4¾ x 4¾in)
Fabric for strap: 3 strips of fabric 1m x 7cm (39½ x 2¾in) (these can be pieces joined together from scraps of fabric)
Lining and interfacing for purse: 15 x 19cm (6 x 7½in)

TENSION (GAUGE)
16 sts x 27 rows over 10 x 10cm (4 x 4in) in moss stitch

FINISHED SIZE
Bag: 22 x 20cm (8¾ x 8in) excluding strap
Purse: 12 x 8cm (4¾ x 3in)

STRAP

With the three long strips of fabric, or joined pieces making up the length required, press each piece down the centre, then fold the sides in to the centre and pin in place. Fold over the top and bottom edges and pin in place. Machine sew the long and short edges.

Pin the top edges of the three pieces together on top of each other, and hand sew in place. Make a braid, pinning and hand sewing the bottom edge when it is finished.

COIN PURSE

Using yarn A, cast on 18 sts.
Row 1: *k1, p1; rep from * to end.
Row 2: *p1, k1; rep from * to end.
Repeat these 2 rows until work measures 16cm (6¼in). Cast off.

BLOCKING

Block and press all bag and purse pieces with a damp cloth (see page 115).

EMBROIDERY

Do this before lining and making up the bag. Embroider the flowers using French knots (see page 110) and lazy daisy stitch (see page 111) with yarns C to G on both the bag and the knitted pocket (place the pocket on the bag and mark with pins to avoid embroidering flowers behind it). Using yarn G, embroider the top of the knitted pocket with blanket stitch (see page 110).

Sew the side seams of the bag together using mattress stitch (see page 117). Pin the strap into place and sew it on. Using yarn G, embroider blanket stitch around the top edge of the bag.

MAKING UP

Cut out the lining fabric and wadding/batting for the main bag, lining and interfacing for the pocket, according to the measurements given. The amount of fabric given for the lining includes the extra needed for the flap.

Turn under a seam allowance of 1.5cm (⁵⁄₈ in) for the flap piece and machine sew to form the shape of the flap. Make the fabric pocket according to the lining instructions on page 122, placing the pocket below the back flap.

Pin a seam allowance of 1.5cm (⁵⁄₈ in) for the other end of the bag lining in place, pin the side seams with RS facing and try it inside the bag for fit, pinning around the top to check. Make sure that it fits well and adjust if needed. Machine stitch the top and side seams with RS facing.

Pin the lining into the bag, making sure the back flap lining sits neatly on the knitted flap. Hand sew in place.

Sew on snap fasteners (see page 120) to the bottom of the flap and the main bag where the flap closes. Sew buttons (see page 119) on the bottom of the outside of the flap over the snap fasteners.

MAKING UP THE PURSE

Follow the instructions on pages 118 and 122 to insert the zip and lining.

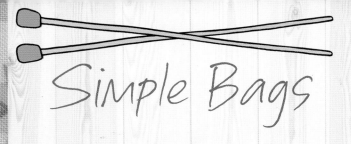

Simple Bags

LEAVES

 Intermediate

A chunky yarn makes the leaves in this pattern into large-scale motifs. The top is finished in rib, and the handles used are made from a colourful braided-effect plastic.

INSTRUCTIONS

FRONT AND BACK (MAKE 2)
Cast on 36 sts.
Row 1: purl.
Row 2: knit.
Start pattern.
Row 3 (RS): p7, *M1, k1, M1, p6, rep from * to last st, p1 (44 sts).
Row 4: k1, *k6, p3, rep from * to last 7 sts, k7.
Row 5: p7, *k1, yf, k1, yf, k1, p6, rep from * to last st, p1 (52 sts).
Row 6: k1, *k6, p5, rep from * to last 7 sts, k7.
Row 7: p7, *k2, yf, k1, yf, k2, p6, rep from * to last st, p1 (60 sts).
Row 8: k1, *k6, p7, rep from * to last 7 sts, k7.
Row 9: p7, *k3, yf, k1, yf, k3, p6, rep from * to last st, p1 (68 sts).
Row 10: k1, *k6, p9, rep from * to last 7 sts, k7.
Row 11: p7, *sl1, k1, psso, k5, k2tog, p6, rep from * to last st, p1 (60 sts).
Row 12: k1, *k6, p7, rep from * to last 7 sts, k7.
Row 13: p7, *sl1, k1, psso, k3, k2tog, p6, rep from * to last st, p1 (52 sts).
Row 14: k1, *k6, p5, rep from * to last 7 sts, k7.
Row 15: p7, *sl1, k1, psso, k1, k2tog, p6, rep from * to last st, p1 (44 sts).

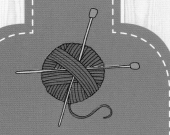

Equipment

KNITTING NEEDLES

10mm (UK 000, US 15)

MATERIALS

3 balls of super chunky (super bulky) yarn in green; 100g/80m/87yd

Handles: plaited plastic with ring attachments, 60cm (23¾in) long

25mm (1in) wooden button

Snap fastener

Lining and interfacing: 40 x 73cm (15¾ x 28¾in)

Lining for pocket: 18 x 33cm (7 x 13in)

Interfacing for pocket: 15 x 15cm (6 x 6in)

TENSION (GAUGE)

9 sts x 14 rows over 10 x 10cm (4 x 4in) in reverse st st

FINISHED SIZE

37 x 35cm (14½ x 13¾in) excluding handles

Row 16: k1, *k6, p3, rep from * to last 7 sts, k7.
Row 17: p7, *sl1, k2tog, psso, p6, rep from * to last st, p1 (36 sts).
Rows 18, 20 and 22: knit.
Rows 19 and 21: purl.
Rows 3–22 form the pattern. Repeat once more.
Next row: *k2, p2, rep from * to end.
Rep this row four more times.
Cast off.

TAB
Cast on 6 sts.
Row 1: k2, p2, k2.
Row 2: p2, k2, p2.
Rep last 2 rows three more times. Cast off.

MAKING UP

Block and press the edges of the bag pieces under a damp cloth (see page 115). Pin the bottom of the bag right sides together and sew the seam using backstitch (see page 116). Then sew the side seams using mattress stitch (see page 117). Pin the tab to the centre back of the bag and sew in place.

Sew the snap fastener (see page 120) to the tab and the front of the bag. Sew on the button (see page 119) to cover the snap fastener on the tab.

To make and attach the lining, follow the instructions on page 122. Place the handles onto the top of the bag and sew around the rings, using the bag yarn to attach them securely.

Summer Bags

BEACH BAG

 *Intermediate*

This colourful cotton bag uses a knot stitch to add texture to the stripes. The strap is made from braided knitted strips, and a matching sunglasses case makes this pair perfect for a day at the beach.

INSTRUCTIONS

FRONT AND BACK (MAKE 2)
Using yarn D, cast on 61 sts.
Row 1: purl.
Start pattern.
Rows 2–5: using yarn D, work 4 rows in st st, starting with a k row.
Row 6: using yarn A, k1, (k1, yf, k1) into next st, *sl1, (k1, yf, k1) into next st, rep from * to last st, k1.
Row 7: using yarn A, k1, k3tog tbl, *sl1, k3tog tbl, rep from * to last st, k1.
Rows 2–7 form the pattern.
Repeat the 6-row pattern, working rows 6 and 7 in yarn A throughout, and rows 2–5 in yarn E, then yarn C, then yarn B, then yarn D.
Continue the 6-row pattern in the given stripe sequence until the third stripe in yarn B is complete, and rows 6 and 7 in yarn A have been worked.
Using yarn D, knit 4 rows.
Cast off.

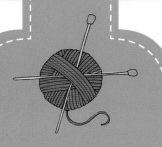

Equipment

KNITTING NEEDLES
4.5mm (UK 7, US 7)

MATERIALS
(Note: amounts are for the bag and sunglasses case)
2 balls of aran (10-ply/worsted) yarn in cream (A), 1 ball each of lilac (B), green (C), turquoise (D) and pink (E); 50g/85m/92yd
Magnetic closure
Lining and wadding/batting for bag: 33 x 50cm (13 x 19¾in)
Lining for pocket: 15 x 27cm (6 x 10¾in)
Interfacing for pocket: 12 x 12cm (4¾ x 4¾in)
Lining and wadding/batting for sunglasses case: 19 x 23cm (7½ x 9in)

TENSION (GAUGE)
20 sts x 32 rows over 10 x 10cm (4 x 4in) in pattern

FINISHED SIZE
Bag: 30 x 23cm (11¾ x 9in) excluding strap
Sunglasses case: 17 x 10cm (6½ x 4in)

STRAP BRAID (MAKE 3)

Using yarn A, cast on 5 sts.
Work in st st until work measures 42cm (16½in).
Cast off.

SUNGLASSES CASE

Using yarn D, cast on 41 sts.
Row 1: purl.
Follow 6-row pattern as for bag until the second stripe in yarn B is complete, and rows 6 and 7 have been worked.
Next row (RS): using yarn D, knit.
Eyelet row: k4, *k2tog, yf, k4, rep from * to last 7 sts, k2tog, yf, k5.
Knit 2 rows.
Cast off.

FLOWER

Using yarn B, cast on 49 sts.
Row 1: knit.
Row 2: purl.
Row 3: k1, (k2, pass 1st st over 2nd st) to end (25 sts).
Row 4: p2tog to last st, p1 (13 sts).
Row 5: k1, (k2tog) six times (7 sts).
Thread yarn through remaining sts.
Fasten off.

MAKING UP

Block and press the bag pieces under a dry cloth (see page 115). Pin the bottom of the bag right sides together and sew the seam using backstitch (see page 116). Then sew the side seams using mattress stitch (see page 117).

Sew the three pieces of the strap together at the top edge, with RS facing up. Braid together, keeping the RS facing up. Sew the bottom edges together. Pin the completed strap to the top of the side seams of the bag and sew in place. Pin the flower to the centre top of the bag and sew it on with yarn B and a tapestry needle (see page 113).

To make and attach the lining, follow the instructions on page 122 and the instructions on page 121 to fit the magnetic closure. The print in this project has a direction, so make the lining and wadding/batting in two pieces, and make sure the lining for the pocket is in the right direction on one side. When sewing the lining to the bag, make sure the end of the handle is tucked into the lining. The lining should start at the bottom of the top border.

When sewing the lining into the sunglasses case, make sure the lining stops just below the eyelets.

TIE FOR SUNGLASSES CASE

Cut two strands each of yarn A, B and C, each one 60cm (23¾in) long. Separate into three groups of two and braid to form a tie, making a knot at each end. Thread the braid through the eyelets and tie in a bow on the outside of the case.

DAISY BASKET

 Beginner

A simple knit and purl stitch in cotton gives this bag the appearance of a woven basket. The top and handles are worked in garter stitch, and it is finished with rows of fresh white daisies.

INSTRUCTIONS

FRONT AND BACK (MAKE 2)
Using yarn A held double and 4.5mm (UK 7, US 7) needles, cast on 53 sts.
Row 1 (RS): k7, *p3, k6; rep from * to last 10 sts, p3, k7.
Row 2: p7, *k3, p6; rep from * to last 10 sts, k3, p7.
Repeat these 2 rows twice more.
Row 7: as row 2.
Row 8: as row 1.
Rep the last 2 rows once more.
These 10 rows form the pattern. Rep until 5 repeats in total have been worked.
Knit 10 rows.
Cast off.

HANDLE (MAKE 2)
Using yarn A held double and 4.5mm (UK 7, US 7) needles, cast on 9 sts.
Knit every row until work measures 40cm (15¾in).
Cast off.

Equipment

KNITTING NEEDLES
4.5mm (UK 7, US 7)
4mm (UK 8, US 6)

MATERIALS
5 balls of DK (8-ply/light worsted) yarn in beige (A), 1 ball each in white (B) and yellow (C); 50g/85m/92yd

Magnetic closure

Lining and wadding/batting: 34 x 54cm (13½ x 21¼in)

Lining for pocket: 18 x 33cm (7 x 13in)

Interfacing for pocket: 15 x 15cm (6 x 6in)

TENSION (GAUGE)
16 sts x 24 rows over 10 x 10cm (4 x 4in) on 4.5mm (UK 7, US 7) needles in pattern with yarn held double

FINISHED SIZE
31 x 25cm (12 x 9¾in) excluding handles

FLOWERS

Make 8 flowers in total, with 5 petals for each flower.

PETALS (MAKE 40)

Using yarn B and 4mm (UK 8, US 6) needles with a single strand of yarn, cast on 5 sts.
Knit 6 rows.
Row 7: k2tog, k1, k2tog (3 sts).
Row 8: knit.
Row 9: k2tog, k1 (2 sts).
Row 10: k2tog.
Cast off.

FLOWER CENTRES (MAKE 8)

Using yarn C and 4mm (UK 8, US 6) needles with a single strand of yarn, cast on 6 sts.
Knit 7 rows.
Cast off, leaving one end long enough to gather.
Gather around the edges to form a bobble, leaving a length of yarn to sew on to the bag.

MAKING UP

Block and press the pieces under a damp cloth (see page 115). Choose which side you prefer as the right side – the sample uses the side with more stocking stitch (US stockinette stitch) than garter stitch.

Pin the bottom of the bag right sides together and sew the seam using backstitch (see page 116). Then sew the side seams using mattress stitch (see page 117), and pin and sew the handles to the inside top of the bag.

Pin the petals along the top of the bag, placing four flowers on each side, and sew the wide end of each petal securely to the bag using yarn B – the pointed ends of the petals can be left loose. Place the bobbles at the centre of the flowers, pulling the length of yarn to the back of the bag, and attach securely.

Follow the lining instructions on page 122 to make and fit the lining, and the instructions on page 121 to fit the magnetic closure.

Summer Bags

NAUTICAL

 Beginner

This simple striped bag has a ribbed top which folds over the circular handles. The contrast knitted tie gives it a colourful nautical look.

INSTRUCTIONS

FRONT AND BACK (MAKE 2)
Using yarn A, cast on 47 sts.
Row 1: knit.
Begin stripe sequence.
Row 2: purl in A.
Row 3: knit in A.
Row 4: purl in A.
Row 5: knit in A.
Row 6: purl in B.
Row 7: knit in B.
Continue to work in st st, working the 6-row stripe sequence until 9 repeats in total have been worked.
Using yarn A, p 1 row, dec 1 st in centre (46 sts).
Eyelet row: k5, (k2tog, yf, k5) five times, k2tog, yf, k4.
Using yarn A, work rib as follows:
Rib row 1: *k2, p2, rep from * to last 2 sts, k2.
Rib row 2: *p2, k2, rep from * to last 2 sts, p2.
Continue in rib for 4 more rows.
Change to yarn B.
Work 2 rows rib.
Change to yarn A.
Work 6 rows rib.
Cast off.

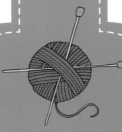

Equipment

KNITTING NEEDLES

4.5mm (UK 7, US 7)

MATERIALS

2 balls of aran (10-ply/worsted) yarn in cream (A), 1 ball each in dark blue (B) and red (C); 50g/85m/92yd

Handles: pair of white plastic circles, 13cm (5¼in) in diameter

Lining and wadding/batting: 28 x 55cm (11 x 21¾in)

Lining for pocket: 13 x 23cm (5 x 9in)

Interfacing for pocket: 10 x 10cm (4 x 4in)

TENSION (GAUGE)

17 sts x 26 rows over 10 x 10cm (4 x 4in) in st st

FINISHED SIZE

27 x 26cm (10¾ x 10¼in) excluding handles

TIE
Using yarn C, cast on 135 sts.
Knit 3 rows.
Cast off.

MAKING UP

Block and press the bag pieces under a dry cloth
(see page 115). Pin the bottom of the bag right sides
together and sew the seam using backstitch (see
page 116). Sew the side seams 20cm (8in) up from the
bottom of the bag using mattress stitch (see page 117),
leaving the rest open at the top.

To make and attach the lining, follow the instructions
on page 122. Pin and sew the lining to just below the
eyelets, turning under the sides of the lining at the top
where the sides are left open. Turn the top of the rib
border over the handles, with the yarn B stripe at the
top. Sew in place, leaving the sides open at the top.

Thread the tie though the eyelets, threading the tie
so that it is on the inside at the sides, and leaving the
sides loose to open the bag.

BOHEMIAN

 Intermediate

This folk-inspired bag is knitted in the round in a cotton yarn. It is embellished with an appliqué flower, embroidery and wooden beads. The tie and strap are braided in different-coloured strands of yarn.

INSTRUCTIONS

NOTES

The bag is made in one piece starting with the circular base and working in the round. You may find it easier to work the first few rounds on double-pointed needles rather than the circular needle.

BAG

Using 4mm (UK 8, US 6) circular needles or DPN and yarn A, cast on 4 sts and join in the round, taking care not to twist stitches. Place marker for beginning of round.

Round 1: kfb four times (8 sts).
Round 2: kfb eight times (16 sts).
Round 3: knit.
Round 4: *k1, kfb; rep from * to end (24 sts).
Rounds 5 and 6: knit.
Round 7: *k1, kfb, k1; rep from * to end (32 sts).
Rounds 8 and 9: knit.
Round 10: *kfb, k2, kfb; rep from * to end (48 sts).
Rounds 11 and 12: knit.
Round 13: *k1, kfb, k2, kfb, k1; rep from * to end (64 sts).
Rounds 14–16: knit.
Round 17: *k1, kfb, k4, kfb, k1; rep from * to end (80 sts).
Rounds 18–20: knit.
Round 21: *k2, kfb, k4, kfb, k2; rep from * to end (96 sts).
Rounds 22–25: knit.
Round 26: *k1, kfb, k3, kfb, k3, kfb, k2; rep from * to end (120 sts).
Round 27: knit.
Round 28: purl.
The base is now complete.

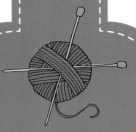

Equipment

KNITTING NEEDLES

4mm (UK 8, US 6)
4mm (UK 8, US 6) circular needles
4mm (UK 8, US 6) DPN (optional)

MATERIALS

3 balls of DK (8-ply/light worsted) yarn in cream (A), 1 ball each in rust (B), pink (C), yellow (D) and green (E); 50g/85m/93yd
Stitch marker
Lining and wadding/batting: sides (one piece): 64 x 23cm (25½ x 9in), base: 22cm (8¾in) diameter circle
Lining for pocket: 18 x 33cm (7 x 13in)
Interfacing for pocket: 15 x 15cm (6 x 6in)
10 4mm (¼in) diameter wooden beads

TENSION (GAUGE)

22 sts x 28 rows over 10 x 10cm (4 x 4in) in st st

FINISHED SIZE

19 x 25cm (7½ x 9¾in) excluding strap

Change to yarn B and knit 9 rounds.
Change to yarn A and knit 49 rounds.
Eyelet round: *k2, k2tog, yf, k2; rep from * to end.
Next round: knit.
Change to yarn B.
Next round: knit.
Next round: purl.
Rep last 2 rounds four more times, decreasing one st at the end of the final round (119 sts).
Change to yarn A and cast off as follows:
Cast off 2 sts, *sl remaining st back to LH needle, cast on 2 sts, cast off 4 sts, rep from * to last st, sl remaining st back to LH needle, cast on 2 sts, cast off 3 sts. Fasten off.

FLOWER PETALS (MAKE 6)

Using yarn C and 4mm (UK 8, US 6) needles, cast on 1 st.
Row 1: kfbf (3 sts).
Row 2 and all WS rows: sl1, p to end.
Row 3: sl1, m1, k1, m1, k1 (5 sts).
Row 5: sl1, m1, k3, m1, k1 (7 sts).
Rows 7 and 9: sl1, k to end.
Row 11: sl1, ssk, k1, k2tog, k1 (5 sts).
Row 13: sl1, sl2, k1, pass 2 slipped sts over, k1 (3 sts).
Row 15: sl1, k2tog, pass slipped st over and fasten yarn off.

FLOWER CENTRE

Using yarn D and 4mm (UK 8, US 6) needles, cast on 4 sts and work rounds 1–3 of bag. Cast off all sts.

APPLIQUÉ AND EMBROIDERY

Pin the flower centre to the bag 10cm (4in) up from the base at the front of the bag (i.e. the fabric pocket should be at the back, and slightly to the right). Hand sew in place (see page 109). Pin the petals around the flower centre and sew in place all round the edges of each petal using yarn C.

Using yarn E and the photograph for guidance, embroider the swirling stems around the flower in chain stitch (see page 111).

Using yarn D, embroider 10 French knots (see page 110) along the bottom border. Using yarn C, embroider lazy daisy stitch petals (see page 111) around the French knot centres. Sew the wooden beads on to the top border, spacing them evenly.

MAKING UP

Cut a circle of lining and wadding/batting to the correct size for the base of the bag. Cut a long rectangle of lining and wadding/batting for the main part of the bag. Make the pocket according to the lining instructions on page 122.

Pin the side seam of the main piece, and pin this tubular piece onto the circular base. Place into the bag to see that it fits. The lining should end just below the eyelets. Adjust if necessary. Sew the seam of the main piece then the two pieces together, making sure that the pocket sits at the centre back. Pin the lining to the bag and sew in place by hand, making sure the lining sits just below the eyelets.

TIE

Cut nine strands of yarn in mixed colours, each one 90cm (35½in) long. Separate into three groups of three and braid to form a tie, making a knot at each end. Thread the tie through the eyelets, bringing both ends out of the same eyelet where they meet, and tie a knot so they hang down the side of the bag.

STRAP

Cut 15 strands of yarn in mixed colours, each one 1m (39½in) long (or adjust to the length you prefer – remember that the resulting braid will be shorter when finished). Separate into three groups of five and braid to form a strap, making a knot at each end. Pin it onto the outside of the bag at the top where the rust band is and sew in place.

Cablework

WAVES & PODS

 *Advanced*

The wave and pod cables that decorate this bag give it a coastal quality, and the soft yarn helps to create an interesting texture. The top of the bag is worked in rib, with chunky wooden beaded handles to add a bit of drama.

INSTRUCTIONS

FRONT AND BACK (MAKE 2)
Cast on 55 sts.
Row 1 (WS): k3, (p4, k1, kfb, k2, kfb, k1, p5, k2) three times, k1 (61 sts).
Row 2 (RS): p3, (k5, p6, Tw5B, k1tbl, p2) three times, p1.
Row 3 (WS): k3, (p1, k2, p3, k6, p5, k2) three times, k1.
Row 4: p3, (k1, sl2, k1, p2sso, k1, p4, Tw5B, p2, k1tbl, p2), three times, p1 (55 sts).
Row 5: k3, (p1, k4, p3, k4, p3, k2) three times, k1.
Row 6: p3, (sl2, k1, p2sso, p2, Tw5B, p4, CDI, p2) three times, p1.
Row 7: k3, (p3, k6, p3, k2, p1, k2) three times, k1.
Row 8: p3, (k1tbl, Tw5B, p6, k1, CDI, k1, p2) three times, p1 (61 sts).
Row 9: k3, (p5, k8, p4, k2) three times, k1.
Row 10: p3, (k4, p8, k5, p2) three times, p1.
Row 11: rep row 9.
Row 12: p3, (k1tbl, Tw5F, p6, k5, p2) three times, p1.
Row 13: k3, (p5, k6, p3, k2, p1, k2) three times, k1.
Row 14: p3, (k1tbl, p2, Tw5F, p4, k1, sl2, k1, p2sso, k1, p2) three times, p1 (55 sts).
Row 15: k3, (p3, k4, p3, k4, p1, k2) three times, k1.

Equipment

KNITTING NEEDLES
6mm (UK 4, US 10)
Cable needle

MATERIALS
7 balls of chunky (bulky) yarn in grey; 50g/50m/54yd

Handles: two chunky wooden beaded

Lining and interfacing: 36 x 73cm (14 x 28¾in)

Lining for pocket: 18 x 33cm (7 x 13in)

Interfacing for pocket: 15 x 15cm (6 x 6in)

TENSION (GAUGE)
16 sts x 19 rows to 10 x 10cm (4 x 4in) in st st

FINISHED SIZE
33 x 40cm (13 x 15¾in) excluding handles

Row 16: p3, (CDI, p4, Tw5F, p2, sl2, k1, p2sso, p2) three times, p1.

Row 17: k3, (p1, k2, p3, k6, p3, k2) three times, k1.

Row 18: p3, (k1, CDI, k1, p6, Tw5F, k1tbl, p2) three times, p1 (61 sts).

Row 19: k3, (p4, k8, p5, k2) three times, k1.

Row 20: p3, (k5, p8, k4, p2), three times, p1.

Row 21: rep row 19.

Rep rows 2–21 and then rows 2–15 again.

Row 56: p2tog, p1, (CDI, p4, Tw5F, p2, sl2, k1, p2sso, p2) twice, CDI, p4, Tw5F, p2, sl2, k1, p2sso, p1, p2tog (53 sts).

Row 57: k2, (p1, k2, p3, k6, p3, k2) three times.

Row 58: p2tog, (k1, CDI, k1, p6, Tw5F, k1tbl, p2) twice, k1, CDI, k1, p6, Tw5F, k1tbl, p2tog (57 sts).

Row 59: k1, (p4, k8, p5, k2) twice, p4, k8, p5, k1.

Row 60: p1, (k5, p8, k4, p2tog) twice, k5, p8, k4, p1 (55 sts).

Row 61: k1, (p4, k8, p5, k1) three times.

Row 62: k2tog, k1, *p1, k1, rep from * to last 2 sts, k2tog (53 sts).

Row 63: p2, *k1, p1, rep from * to last st, p1.

Row 64: k2, *p1, k1, rep from * to last st, k1.

Row 65: p2, *k1, p1, rep from * to last st, p1.

Rep rows 64 and 65 until rib measures 10cm (4in).

Cast off in rib.

MAKING UP

Block and press the edges of the bag under a damp cloth (see page 115). Pin the bottom of the bag right sides together and sew the seam using backstitch (see page 116). Then sew the side seams using mattress stitch (see page 117). Fold the top of the rib in half and slip stitch in place.

To make and attach the lining, follow the instructions on page 122. Pin the lining to just below the rib. Sew the handles securely in place on the rib, using the same yarn as used for the bag.

Cablework

BOBBLES & WAVES

 *Advanced*

A tweedy yarn with a simple cable at the centre and repeated bobbles and waves make an interesting surface texture. The bag is finished with moss stitch for the border and shoulder strap.

INSTRUCTIONS

Note: Hold yarn double throughout.

WAVES RIGHT (8 STS)
Row 1 (RS): p4, Tw3B, p1.
Row 2 (WS): k2, p2, k4.
Row 3: p3, Tw3B, p2.
Row 4: k3, p2, k3.
Row 5: p2, Tw3B, p3.
Row 6: k2, MB, k1, p2, k2.
Row 7: p2, Tw3F, p3.
Row 8: rep row 4.
Row 9: p3, Tw3F, p2.
Row 10: rep row 2.
Row 11: p4, Tw3F, p1.
Row 12: k1, p2, k1, MB, k3.

WAVES LEFT (8 STS)
Row 1 (RS): p1, Tw3F, p4.
Row 2 (WS): k4, p2, k2.
Row 3: p2, Tw3F, p3.
Row 4: k3, p2, k3.
Row 5: p3, Tw3F, p2.
Row 6: k2, p2, k1, MB, k2.
Row 7: p3, Tw3B, p2.
Row 8: rep row 4.

Row 9: p2, Tw3B, p3.
Row 10: rep row 2.
Row 11: p1, Tw3B, p4.
Row 12: k3, mb, k1, p2, k1.

CENTRE PANEL (18 STS)
Row 1 (RS): p6, C6B, p6.
Row 2 (WS): k6, p6, k6.
Row 3: p4, Tw5B, Tw5F, p4.
Row 4: k4, p3, k4, p3, k4.
Row 5: p2, Tw5B, p4, Tw5F, p2.
Row 6: k2, p3, k8, p3, k2.
Row 7: p2, k3, p8, k3, p2.
Row 8: rep row 6.
Row 9: p2, Tw5F, p4, Tw5B, p2.
Row 10: rep row 4.
Row 11: p4, Tw5F, Tw5B, p4.
Row 12: rep row 2.

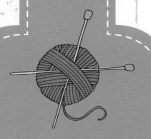

Equipment

KNITTING NEEDLES

4.5mm (UK 7, US 7)

MATERIALS

6 balls of DK (8-ply/light worsted) yarn in blue; 50g/135m/147yd

Cable needle

Snap fastener

2.5cm (1in) button

Lining and wadding/batting: 39 x 63cm (15½ x 25in)

Lining for pocket: 18 x 18cm (7 x 7in)

Interfacing for pocket: 15 x 15cm (6 x 6in)

TENSION (GAUGE)

23 sts x 25 rows over 10 x 10cm (4 x 4in) in cable pattern with yarn held double

FINISHED SIZE

36 x 31cm (14 x 12in) excluding handles

Cablework

FRONT AND BACK (MAKE 2)

Cast on 76 sts using two strands of yarn.

Set-up row (WS): k10, p2, k6, p2, k6, p2, k7, p6, k7, p2, k6, p2, k6, p2, k10.

Row 1 (RS): p5, work row 1 of waves right pattern three times, work row 1 of centre panel, work row 1 of waves left pattern three times, p5.

Row 2 (WS): k5, work row 2 of waves left pattern three times, work row 2 of centre panel, work row 2 of waves right pattern three times, p5.

These two rows set position of pattern. Cont in pattern, dec 1 st each edge on every sixth and twelfth row of pattern, until five reps of pattern are complete. Work a further 10 rows in pattern, decreasing at each edge on the sixth row of pattern (54 sts).

Work top border as follows:

Next row: *k1, p1; rep from * to end.
Next row: *p1, k1; rep from * to end.
These two rows form moss st. Cont as set until moss st band measures 5cm (2in).
Cast off.

HANDLE (MAKE 2)

Cast on 10 sts.
Work in moss st as for top border for 80cm (31½in).
Cast off.

TAB

Cast on 7 sts.
Row 1: *k1, p1; rep from * to last st, k1.
The last row forms moss st.
Continue in moss st until tab measures 5cm (2in).
Cast off.

MAKING UP

Block all pieces and press the edges of the main piece, the handles and the tab under a dry cloth (see page 115).

Pin the bottom of the bag right sides together and sew the seam using backstitch (see page 116). Then sew the side seams using mattress stitch (see page 117). Pin the ends of the handles to the inside of the top of the bag, and sew in place.

Pin the tab to the top centre back of the bag and sew in place. Sew the snap fastener (see page 120) to the tab and the front of the bag. Sew the button (see page 119) to cover the snap fastener on the tab. To make and attach the lining, follow the instructions on page 122.

Cablework

ROPE CABLE

 *Advanced*

The cable for this bag has an intricate twist giving it the appearance of a knotted rope. The wooden rings with the ribbed handles give it a retro look.

INSTRUCTIONS

ROPE CABLE PATTERN (26 STS)
Row 1 (RS): p5, C6F, p4, C6F, p5.
Row 2 (WS): k5, p6, k4, p6, k5.
Row 3: p3, (Tw5B, Tw5F) twice, p3.
Row 4: k3, p3, k4, p6, k4, p3, k3.
Row 5: p2, Tw4B, p4, C6B, p4, Tw4F, p2.
Row 6: k2, p3, k5, p6, k5, p3, k2.
Row 7: p1, Tw4B, p5, k6, p5, Tw4F, p1.
Row 8: k1, p3, k6, p6, k6, p3, k1.
Row 9: p1, Tw4F, p5, k6, p5, Tw4B, p1.
Row 10: rep row 6.
Row 11: p2, Tw4F, p4, C6B, p4, Tw4B, p2.
Row 12: rep row 4.
Row 13: p3, (Tw5F, Tw5B) twice, p3.
Row 14: rep row 2.
Row 15: p5, C6F, p4, C6F, p5.
Row 16: rep row 2.
Row 17: p5, k3, Tw5F, Tw5B, k3, p5.
Row 18: k5, p3, k2, p6, k2, p3, k5.
Row 19: p5, Tw5F, C6B, Tw5B, p5.
Row 20: k7, p12, k7.
Row 21: p7, C6F twice, p7.
Row 22: rep row 20.
Row 23: p5, Tw5B, C6B, Tw5F, p5.
Row 24: rep row 18.
Row 25: p5, k3, Tw5B, Tw5F, k3, p5.
Row 26: rep row 2.

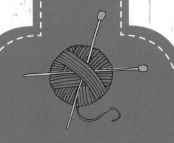

Equipment

KNITTING NEEDLES

5mm (UK 6, US 8)
Cable needle

MATERIALS

6 balls of aran (10-ply/worsted) yarn in stone; 50g/87m/95yd

4 5.5cm (2¼in) diameter wooden or plastic curtain rings

Large snap fastener

25mm (1in) diameter button

Lining and wadding/batting: 39 x 75cm (15½ x 29½in)

Lining and interfacing for pocket: 18 x 33cm (7 x 13in)

TENSION (GAUGE)

Cable pattern: one repeat measures 8.5 x 10cm (3¼ x 4in)

FINISHED SIZE

36 x 36cm (14 x14in) excluding handles

FRONT AND BACK (MAKE 2)

Cast on 92 sts.

Set up row (WS): k9, p6, k4, p6, k13, p6, k4, p6, k13, p6, k4, p6, k9.

Row 1 (RS): p4, (work row 1 of cable pattern, p3) three times, p1.

Row 2: k4, (work row 2 of cable pattern, k3) three times, k1.

These two rows set pattern. Cont as set until two full repeats of pattern plus 20 rows are complete.

Row 73: p2, p2tog, work cable pattern, p1, p2tog, (work cable pattern, p2tog, p1) twice, p1 (88 sts).

Row 74: k3, (work cable pattern, k2) three times, k1.

Row 75: p3, (work cable pattern, p2) three times, p1.

Row 76: k3, (work cable pattern, k2) three times, k1.

Row 77: p1, p2tog, (work cable pattern, p2tog) three times, p1 (84 sts).

Row 78: k2, (work cable pattern, k1) three times, k1.

Row 79: k2tog, k1, *p2, k2, rep from * to last five sts, p2, k1, k2tog (82 sts).

Row 80: p2, *k2, p2, rep from * to end.

Row 81: k2, *p2, k2, rep from * to end.

Rep rows 80 and 81 until rib measures 6cm (2½in).

Cast off in rib.

HANDLE (MAKE 2)

Cast on 10 sts.
Row 1: *k2, p2, rep from * to last 2 sts, k2.
Row 2: *p2, k2, rep from * to last 2 sts, p2.
Repeat last 2 rows until handle measures 76cm (30in).
Cast off.

TAB

Cast on 10 sts.
Row 1: *k2, p2, rep from * to last 2 sts, k2.
Row 2: *p2, k2, rep from * to last 2 sts, p2.
Repeat last 2 rows until tab measures 5cm (2in).
Cast off.

MAKING UP

Block and press the edges under a damp cloth
(see page 115). Pin the bottom of the bag right
sides together and sew the seam using backstitch
(see page 116). Then sew the side seams using
mattress stitch (see page 117).

Pin and sew the tab to the top of the bag. Sew on the
snap fastener (see page 120) and button (see page 119).
Fold over the ends of the handles onto the curtain rings
(the rings may have a hook in them – remove this first and
fill or make sure the hole is covered when sewing onto the
bag). Sew the ends of the handles to the rings. Place the
rings onto the rib border of the bag and sew on securely
with the yarn used for making the bag.

To make and attach the lining, follow the instructions
on page 122.

Cablework

GRAPES & BOBBLES

 *Intermediate*

Chunky bunches of grapes and a bobble border make a unique pattern for this attractive bag. The wooden handles give it a retro look and make it a good project bag for your knitting.

INSTRUCTIONS

The grape motif pattern starts on row 15 of the main pattern (see page 74).

GRAPE MOTIF PATTERN (13 STS)
Row 1 (RS): p6, MB, p6.
Row 2 (WS): knit.
Row 3: purl.
Row 4: knit.
Row 5: p4, MB, p3, MB, p4.
Rows 6–8: as rows 2–4.
Row 9: p2, (MB, p3) twice, MB, p2.
Rows 10–12: as rows 2–4.
Row 13: (MB, p3) three times, MB.
Row 14: k4, p5, k4.
Row 15: p3, k2tog, (k1, yo) twice, k1, ssk, p3.
Row 16: k3, p7, k3.
Row 17: p2, k2tog, k2, yo, k1, yo, k2, ssk, p2.
Row 18: k2, p9, k2.
Row 19: p1, k2tog, k3, yo, k1, yo, k3, ssk, p1.
Row 20: k1, p11, k1.
Row 21: p1, k1, k2tog, m1p, ssk, yo, k1, yo, k2tog, m1p, ssk, k1, p1.
Row 22: k1, p2, k1, p5, k1, p2, k1.
Row 23: p1, k2tog, m1p, p1, m1p, ssk, k1, k2tog, m1p, p1, m1p, ssk, p1.
Row 24: k5, p3, k5.
Row 25: p5, m1p, sl2 as if to k2tog, k1, psso, m1p, p5.
Row 26: k6, p1, k6.

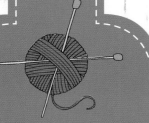

Equipment

KNITTING NEEDLES

5mm (UK 6, US 8)

MATERIALS

2 balls of aran (10-ply/worsted) yarn in beige; 100g/132m/144yd

Handles: wooden D-shaped, 25cm (10in) wide

Lining and wadding/batting: 53 x 31cm (21 x 12in)

Lining for pocket: 15 x 27cm (6 x 10¾in)

Interfacing for pocket: 12 x 12cm (5 x 5in)

TENSION (GAUGE)

17 sts x 26 rows over 10 x 10cm (4 x 4in) in reverse st st

FINISHED SIZE

25 x 23cm (10 x 9in) excluding handles

FRONT AND BACK (MAKE 2)

Cast on 49 sts.

Work 14 rows in rev st st, starting with a p row.

Start pattern motifs:

Next row: (RS) p8, (work row 1 of motif, p7) twice, p1.

Next row: K8, (work row 2 of motif, k7) twice, k1.

These two rows set motif position, continue until motifs are complete.

Work 11 rows more in rev st st.

Next row: knit.

Start border:

Next row: knit.

Cont to k every row until g st section measures approximately 1.5cm (⁵/₈in), ending with a WS row.

Next row: k4, *MB, k3; rep from * to last 5 sts, MB, k4.

Cont in g st until border measures 5cm (2in).

Cast off.

MAKING UP

Block and press the bag pieces under a damp cloth (see page 115). Pin and sew the bottom seam together using mattress stitch (see page 117). Pin the side seam up to 17cm (6½in) from the bottom of the bag and sew, leaving a gap at the top. Insert the garter stitch top edging through the hole in the wooden handle, and pull half of it through. Pin it, then slip stitch it into place.

Cut out the lining fabric and wadding/batting for the bag and pin together. Cut out the lining and interfacing for the pocket. Fold over the seam allowance at the top of one side of the bag and machine stitch in place.

Press the lining fabric for the pocket right sides together, then iron the interfacing onto the pocket. Sew one side and the top of the pocket, clip the corner, turn right sides out and press again, Pin a 1.5cm (⅝in) seam allowance for the open side. Pin it to the lining a little below the centre top and sew the pocket in place. Sew the side seams of the lining, leaving a gap at the top to correspond with the gap at the top of the knitted piece. On the open section of the lining, turn the edges over by 1.5cm (⅝in) and machine stitch in place.

Pin the lining into the bag, checking that it fits correctly, and placing it to slightly cover the seam at the top where the border has been folded over and stitched in place. Hand sew the lining in place.

Evening

LACY LATTICE

 *Intermediate*

Pure silk and fine silk mohair are combined for this delicate bag. The main part is an open lattice lace, finished with a pretty garter stitch border, picot edge and ribbon tie. There is a co-ordinating compact case.

INSTRUCTIONS

FRONT AND BACK (MAKE 2)

Using yarn A and 3.75mm (UK 9, US 5) needles, cast on 45 sts.

Row 1 (RS): k2, *yfrn, p1, p3tog, p1, yo, k1, rep from * to last st, k1.

Row 2 (and every even row): k1, p to last st, k1.

Row 3: k3, yf, sl1, k2tog, psso, yf, *k3, yf, sl1, k2tog, psso, yf, rep from * to last 3 sts, k3.

Row 5: k1, p2tog, p1, yo, k1, yfrn, p1, *p3tog, p1, yo, k1, yfrn, p1, rep from * to last 3 sts, p2tog, k1.

Row 7: k1, k2tog, yf, k3, yf, *sl1, k2tog, psso, yf, k3, yf, rep from * to last 3 sts, sl1, k1, psso, k1.

Row 8: k1, p to last st, k1.

These 8 rows form the lacy lattice stitch pattern.

Repeat nine more times.

Knit 2 rows.

Eyelet row: k4, (k2tog, yf, k4) six times, k2tog, yo, k3.

Next row: k, dec 1 st at centre of row (44 sts).

Change to yarn B.

Using yarn B held double and 4mm (UK 8, US 6) needles, work in g st for 16 rows.

Change to yarn A.

Using yarn A held singly and 3.75mm (UK 9, US 5) needles, picot cast-off as follows: cast off 2 sts, *sl st on RH needle to LH needle, cast on 2 sts, cast off 4 sts, rep from * to end and fasten off remaining st.

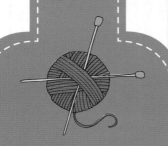

Equipment

KNITTING NEEDLES

3.75mm (UK 9, US 5)
4mm (UK 8, US 6)

MATERIALS

(NB: the yarn amounts will make the bag and the case)

2 balls of DK (8-ply/light worsted) yarn in silver (A); 50g/100m/109yd

1 ball of 1–3-ply (lace weight) mohair/silk yarn in silver (B); 25g/200m/219yd

Ribbon for bag: 75cm (29½in)

Ribbon for compact case: 50cm (19¾in)

Lining and interfacing for bag: 26 x 57cm (10¼ x 22½in)

Lining and interfacing for pocket: 15 x 27cm (6 x 10¾in)

Lining and interfacing for compact case: 14 x 27cm (5½ x 10¾in)

TENSION (GAUGE)

20 sts x 36 rows over 10 x 10cm (4 x 4in) lacy lattice pattern on 3.75mm (UK 9, US 5) needles with DK (8-ply/light worsted) yarn

FINISHED SIZE

Bag: 23 x 27cm (9 x 10¾in) excluding strap

Compact case: 11 x 12cm (4¼ x 4¾in)

COMPACT CASE
Front and back (make 2)
Using yarn A and 3.75mm (UK 9, US 5) needles,
cast on 21 sts.
Work in lacy lattice stitch (rows 1–8) as for bag, until
4 repeats have been worked.
Knit 2 rows.
Eyelet row: k3, (k4, k2tog, yf) four times, k4, yf, k2.
Change to yarn B, held double, and 4mm (UK 8,
US 6) needles.
Work 6 rows g st.
Change to yarn A held singly and 3.75mm (UK 9,
US 5) needles.
Knit 1 row, dec 1 st at centre of row (20 sts).
Work picot cast-off as for bag.

MAKING UP
Block and press all pieces under a dry cloth (see
page 115). Pin the bottom of the bag right sides
together and sew the seam using backstitch
(see page 116). Then sew the side seams using
mattress stitch (see page 117). To make and
attach the lining, follow the instructions on page
122. Line the compact case in the same way,
omitting the pocket.

STRAP

Cut 12 lengths of yarn A, 60cm (23¾in) long. Separate into three lots of four strands and braid them to form a strap, making a knot at each end.

Sew securely onto the top inside of the bag over the seam using matching sewing thread.

TIE

For the bag, cut 75cm (29½in) of ribbon and thread through the eyelets to form a tie.

For the compact case, cut 50cm (19¾in) of ribbon and thread through the eyelets to form a tie.

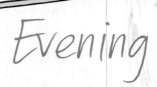

Evening

BUTTERFLY

 *Intermediate*

The mercerised cotton yarn used for this delicate bag adds an extra sheen. The butterfly motif is knitted using intarsia, with added sequins and embroidery. Large sequins embellish the border, and it is finished with a pretty braided tie. See page 108 for more on working the intarsia technique.

INSTRUCTIONS

FRONT AND BACK (MAKE 2)
Using yarn A, cast on 48 sts.
Starting with a RS row, work 6 rows in st st.
Start chart (see page 83), working RS rows in knit, WS rows in purl and the motifs in intarsia.
Row 7 (RS): k10, work chart row 1, k10.
Row 8: p10, work chart row 2, p10.
Continue to follow chart in st st until 25 rows have been worked.
Work 7 rows in st st, starting with a p row.
Change to yarn C.
Knit 5 rows.
Cast off.

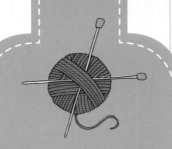

Equipment

KNITTING NEEDLES
4mm (UK 8, US 6)

MATERIALS
1 ball each of DK (8-ply/light worsted) yarn in silver (A), teal (B) and bright pink (C); 50g/130m/142yd

Magnetic closure

14 20mm (¾in) diameter sequins

Selection of 5mm (¼in) diameter multicoloured sequins

Lining and interfacing: 23 x 31cm (9 x 12in)

Lining for pocket: 13 x 15cm (5¼ x 6in)

Interfacing for pocket: 10 x 6cm (4 x 2½in)

TENSION (GAUGE)
22 sts x 28 rows over 10 x 10cm (4 x 4in)

FINISHED SIZE
20 x 14cm (8 x 5½in) excluding strap

MAKING UP

Press pieces under a dry cloth. Using yarn C, embroider the top of the motif in chain stitch (see page 111) to form the butterfly's antennae, and using yarn B make French knots at the top of the antennae (see page 110). Sew the small sequins onto the wings using matching sewing thread, and seven large sequins across each side of the top of the bag, using a single thread of yarn C to attach them. Pin the bottom of the bag right sides together and sew the seam using backstitch (see page 116). Then sew the side seams using mattress stitch (see page 117).

Follow the lining instructions on page 122 to make and fit the lining, and the instructions on page 121 to fit the magnetic closure.

STRAP

Cut 18 strands of yarn C, each 40cm (16in) long. Separate into three groups of six strands and braid to form a strap. Make a knot at each end and attach the strap to the outside top of the bag at either side using yarn C.

Chart for intarsia butterfly pattern

Colour key:

⬜	Yarn A
🟦	Yarn B
🟪	Yarn C

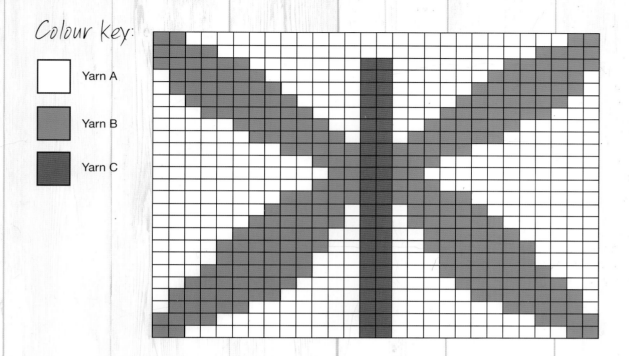

Evening

LACE & RIBBON

 *Intermediate*

The yarn used here is a cotton mix twisted with a metallic thread and sequins. A lace stitch is topped with garter stitch for the border and handles, and tied with a matching velvet ribbon.

INSTRUCTIONS

FRONT AND BACK (MAKE 2)
Cast on 51 sts.
Row 1 (RS): k1, k2tog, k4, yf, k1, yf, k4, *sl1, k2tog, psso, k4, yf, k1, yf, k4, rep from * to last 3 sts, sl1, k1, psso, k1.
Row 2 (and every alternate row): purl.
Row 3: k1, k2tog, k3, (yf, k3) twice, *sl1, k2tog, psso, k3, (yf, k3) twice, rep from * to last 3 sts, sl1, k1, psso, k1.
Row 5: k1, k2tog, k2, yf, k5, yf, k2, *sl1, k2tog, psso, k2, yf, k5, yf, k2, rep from * to last 3 sts, sl1, k1, psso, k1.
Row 7: k2, *yf, k4, sl1, k2tog, psso, k4, yf, k1, rep from * to last st, k1.
Row 9: k3, yf, k3, sl1, k2tog, psso, k3, *(yf, k3) twice, sl1, k2tog, psso, k3, rep from * to last 3 sts, yf, k3.
Row 11: k4, yf, k2, sl1, k2tog, psso, k2, *yf, k5, yf, k2, sl1, k2tog, psso, k2, rep from * to last 4 sts, yf, k4.
Row 12: purl.
These 12 rows form the pattern.
Repeat the 12-row pattern twice more, then rows 1–6 once. Knit 14 rows.
Cast off.

Equipment

KNITTING NEEDLES

4mm (UK 8, US 6)

MATERIALS

2 balls of DK (8-ply/light worsted) yarn in pink; 50g/110m/120yd
Magnetic closure
Velvet ribbon: 1cm x 1m (³/₈ x 39½in)
Lining and interfacing: 29 x 46cm (11½ x 18in)
Lining for pocket: 15 x 27cm (6 x 10¾in)

TENSION (GAUGE)

18 sts x 26 rows over 10 x 10cm (4 x 4in) in pattern

FINISHED SIZE

26 x 20cm (10¼ x 8in) excluding handles

HANDLE (MAKE 2)
Cast on 8 sts.
Knit until handle measures 40cm (15¾in).
Cast off.

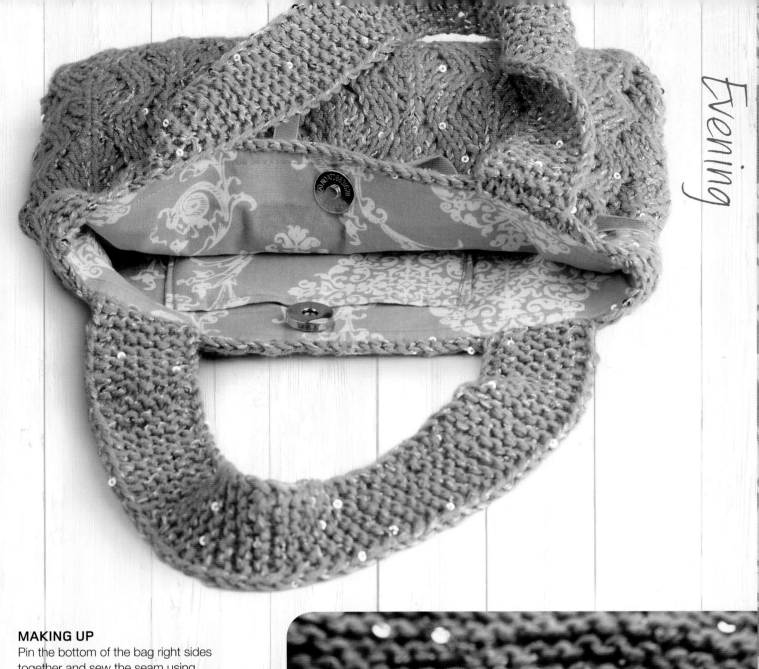

MAKING UP

Pin the bottom of the bag right sides
together and sew the seam using
backstitch (see page 116). Then sew
the side seams using mattress stitch (see
page 117). Pin the handles to the inside
of the bag and sew in place.

Follow the lining instructions on page
122 to fit the lining, and the instructions
on page 121 to fit the magnetic closure.

Thread the ribbon through the top of
the lace section, and tie in a bow at the
front of the bag.

Colourwork

NORDIC

  Intermediate

An all-over Fair Isle in bright colours gives this bag a wintry look. The top and shoulder strap are knitted in rib, and the braided tie is finished with a pair of pompoms. See page 107 in the Techniques section for more on working the Fair Isle technique.

INSTRUCTIONS

Note: when working from the chart (see page 91), knit rows (RS) are read from right to left, and purl rows (WS) are read from left to right.

FRONT AND BACK (MAKE 2)
Using yarn F, cast on 50 sts.
Row 1: purl.
Row 2 (RS): k1 in E, (work chart row 1) three times, k1 in E.
Row 3: p1 in E, (work chart row 2) three times, p1 in E.
Continue to follow chart as set until 24 rows have been completed, working 1 st at each end in st st, using yarn matching first stitch of chart row. Work one more repeat.
Work first 6 rows of chart once more.
Change to yarn A.
Purl 1 row.
Eyelet row (RS): k4, (k2tog, yf, k4) seven times, k4.
Next row: *k2, p2, rep from * to last 2 sts, k2.
Next row: *p2, k2, rep from * to last 2 sts, p2.
Rep these 2 rows twice more.
Purl 1 row.
Change to yarn F.
Cast off.

Equipment

KNITTING NEEDLES
4.5mm (UK 7, US 7)

MATERIALS
2 balls of aran (10-ply/worsted) yarn in white (A), 1 ball of each in turquoise (C), deep red (D) and purple (F); 50g/70m/76yd

1 ball each of aran (10-ply/worsted) yarn in grey (B) and green (E); 50g/75m/82yd

Lining and wadding/batting: 29 x 70cm (11½ x 27½in)

Lining for pocket: 18 x 33cm (7 x 13in)

Interfacing for pocket: 15 x 15cm (6 x 6in)

TENSION (GAUGE)
19 sts x 19 rows over 10 x 10cm (4 x 4in) in Fair Isle pattern

FINISHED SIZE
26 x 34cm (10¼ x 13½in) excluding strap

STRAP

Using yarn A, cast on 8 sts.
Row 1: *k2, p2, rep from * to end.
Last row forms rib. Continue in rib until strap measures 75cm (29½in).
Cast off.

MAKING UP

Block pieces and press under a damp cloth (see page 115). Pin the bottom of the bag right sides together and sew the seam using backstitch (see page 116). Then sew the side seams using mattress stitch (see page 117). Pin the strap to the inside of the bag and sew in place.

To make and attach the lining, follow the instructions on page 122. Make sure that you sew the lining just below the level of the eyelets.

TIE

Cut six lengths of any colour yarn, each 85cm (33½in) long. Separate into three lots of two strands and braid to form a tie, making a knot at each end.

Make two pompoms in yarn B (or the colour of your choice, see page 114), approximately 5cm (2in) in diameter. Attach one pompom to one end of the tie. Thread the other end through the eyelets, and then attach the second pompom.

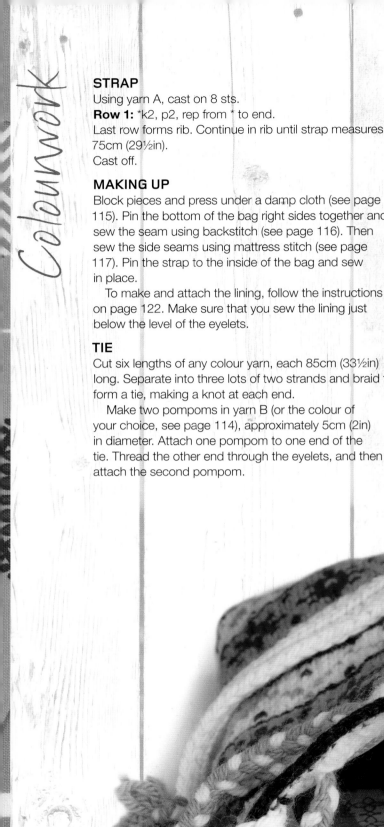

Chart for Fair Isle pattern

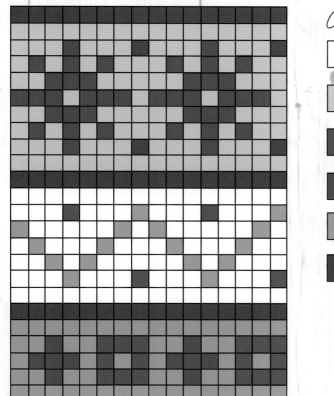

Colour key:

☐ Yarn A

☐ Yarn B

☐ Yarn C

☐ Yarn D

☐ Yarn E

☐ Yarn F

Colourwork

FLOWER FAIR ISLE & RIB

 *Intermediate*

A simple rib in a tweedy yarn forms the main part of this bag. The top has a flower Fair Isle panel with bobbles in rich colours, and it is finished with bamboo handles. See page 107 for more information on working the Fair Isle technique.

INSTRUCTIONS

FRONT AND BACK (MAKE 2)

Using yarn A, cast on 57 sts.
Row 1: k1, *k2, p2, rep from * to last 4 sts, k2, p1, k1.
Rep this row until 56 rows have been worked.
Change to yarn D (use yarn double from now on).
Knit 2 rows.
Change to yarn B.
Work 1 row knit.
Work 1 row purl.
Work from chart (see page 95) as follows, working in st st and starting with a WS row. Use yarn matching first stitch of chart row for first and last stitch. (NB: yarn A on chart is a MB each time, using a single strand of yarn.)
Row 1: k1, (work 16 sts from chart) three times, then first 7 sts once more, k1.
Row 2: p1, (work 16 sts from chart) three times, then first 7 sts once more, p1.
Continue to follow chart, working k1, p1 at beginning and end of row, until 9 rows from the chart have been completed.
Next row: using yarn B, purl.
Next row: using yarn B, knit.
Change to yarn D.
Work 2 rows in knit.
Change to yarn B, and knit 9 rows.
Cast off.

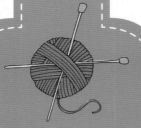

Equipment

KNITTING NEEDLES
4.5mm (UK 7, US 7)

MATERIALS
2 balls of aran (10-ply/worsted) felted tweed yarn in yellow (A); 50g/87m/95yd

1 ball each of DK (8-ply/light worsted) yarn in green (B), red (C) and purple (D); 50g/175m/191yd

Handles: two D-shaped bamboo, 15cm (6in) across at widest point

Lining and wadding/batting: 28 x 63cm (11 x 24¾in)

Lining for pocket: 18 x 33cm (7 x 13in)

Interfacing for pocket: 15 x 15cm (6 x 6in)

Lining for handle casings: 2 pieces 13 x 8cm (5 x 3¼in)

TENSION (GAUGE)
Main: 23 sts x 26 rows over 10 x 10cm (4 x 4in) in rib

Border: 20 sts x 25 rows over 10 x 10cm (4 x 4in) in st st with DK (8-ply/light worsted) used double

FINISHED SIZE
25 x 30cm (9 x 12in) excluding handles

MAKING UP

Block and press the pieces under a damp cloth (see page 115). Pin the bottom of the bag right sides together and sew the seam using backstitch (see page 116). Then sew the side seams using mattress stitch (see page 117). Turn over the top border so that the two knit rows in yarn D are at the top of the border. Slip stitch in place. To make and attach the lining, follow the instructions on page 122. When pinning the lining to the top of the inside of the bag, leave a gap on each side to insert the handle casings.

With the two pieces of fabric for the handle casings, fold the long edges of each piece together, right sides facing, and sew the short sides with 1.5cm (⁵⁄₈in) seam allowance. Clip corners and turn right side out – they will be 10cm (4in) wide. Zigzag the top and bottom edges (these will be inside the lining so will not show).

Place the bottom of the casing inside the lining and pin, then fold the other side over to fit snugly around the handles. Slip stitch in place to complete the lining and secure the handles. Using yarn A, secure the handle in place on either side at the top of the knitted piece on the inside (see inset, below).

Chart for Fair Isle border

Colour Key:

- ⬤ MB Yarn A
- ⬜ Yarn B
- 🟫 Yarn C
- ⬛ Yarn D

Colourwork

AUTUMN

 Intermediate

Large-scale flower and leaf intarsia motifs in a tweed yarn form a rich pattern here. Embroidery and bobbles add embellishment, and the top and handles are worked in moss stitch. The back of the bag is worked in beige and purple stripes. See page 108 for more information on working the intarsia technique.

INSTRUCTIONS

FRONT
Using yarn A, cast on 58 sts.
Row 1: knit.
Start chart (see page 99). Work WS rows in purl and RS rows in knit. Work the motifs in intarsia (see page 108).
Row 1 (WS): p1 in A, work chart row 1, p1 in A.
Row 2: k1 in A, work chart row 2, k1 in A.
Continue as set until 60 rows of chart have been completed.
Moss stitch border (using yarn A only):
Row 1 (WS): *k1, p1; rep from * to end.
Row 2 (RS): *p1, k1; rep from * to end.
The last 2 rows form moss st.
Continue in moss st until 20 rows have been worked.
Cast off.

BACK
Using yarn A, cast on 58 sts.
Row 1: purl.
Working in st st, work stripes as follows:
4 rows in yarn A, 2 rows in yarn B.
Continue until 10 repeats of the 6-row stripe pattern have been worked.
Knit 1 row in yarn A.
Work moss stitch border as for Front.

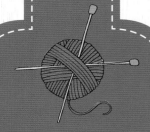

Equipment

KNITTING NEEDLES
4.5mm (UK 7, US 7)

MATERIALS
2 balls of aran (10-ply/worsted) yarn in beige (A), 1 ball each in purple (B), dark green (C) and dark purple (D); 50g/87m/95yd

Small amount of aran (10-ply/worsted) yarn in deep pink (E); 50g/88m/96yd

2cm (¾in) diameter button

Snap fastener

Lining and wadding/batting: 36 x 62cm (14¼ x 24½in)

Lining for pocket: 18 x 33cm (7 x 13in)

Interfacing for pocket: 15 x 15cm (6 x 6in)

TENSION (GAUGE)
16 sts x 24 rows over 10 x 10cm (4 x 4in) in st st

FINISHED SIZE
34 x 29cm (13½ x 11½in) excluding handles

HANDLE (MAKE 2)

Using yarn A, cast on 7 sts.

Row 1: *k1, p1; rep from * to last st, k1.

This row forms moss st.

Continue in moss st until handle measures 40cm (15¾in).

Cast off.

TAB

Using yarn A, cast on 7 sts.

Row 1: *k1, p1; rep from * to last st, k1.

This row forms moss st.

Repeat last row twelve more times.

Cast off.

MAKING UP

Block and press the bag pieces under a damp cloth (see page 115).

Using yarn D and the photograph as a guide, embroider a line of chain stitches (see page 111), starting at the centre of each petal and finishing at the point. With the same yarn, embroider French knots (see page 110) in groups of three as berries.

Pin the bottom of the bag right sides together and sew the seam using backstitch (see page 116). Then sew the side seams using mattress stitch (see page 117). Fold the top moss stitch section in half and slip stitch in place. Pin the handles to the inside top of the bag and sew in place. Sew the button onto the tab and the snap fastener (see page 120) onto the underside of the tab and the front of the bag to correspond.

To make and attach the lining, follow the instructions on page 122.

Chart for intarsia flowers and leaves

Colour key:

⬜	Yarn A
🟩	Yarn B
🟩	Yarn C
◉	MB Yarn E

NB: Yarn D is used for embroidery only

ARGYLE

 *Intermediate*

Chunky yarn and large-scale motifs add impact to this pattern. Bobbles and embroidery are added to the intarsia motifs, and the border and handles are knitted in moss stitch, making an attractive contrast. See page 108 for more information on working the intarsia technique.

INSTRUCTIONS

FRONT AND BACK (MAKE 2)

Using yarn A, cast on 27 sts.
Starting with a RS row, work 3 rows in st st.
Start chart (see page 103). Work WS rows in purl and RS rows in knit.
Row 4 (WS): p2 in A, *work chart row 1, p1 in yarn A, rep from * twice more, p1 in yarn A.
Row 5 (RS): k2 in A, *work chart row 2, k1 in yarn A, rep from * twice more, k1 in yarn A.
Continue to follow chart as set until 19 rows have been completed, working a bobble into the centre stitch of the motif in yarn C, as shown on the chart.
Work 3 rows st st in yarn A.
Next row (WS): *k1, p1; rep from * to last st, k1.
The last row forms moss st.
Work 4 more rows in moss st.
Change to yarn B.
Cast off (RS).

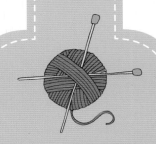

Equipment

KNITTING NEEDLES

8mm (UK 0, US 11)

MATERIALS

2 balls of super chunky (super bulky) yarn in beige (A) and 1 ball in orange (B); 100g/80m/87yd

Small amount of aran (10-ply/worsted) yarn in dark purple (C); 50g/87m/95yd

Small amount of aran (10-ply/worsted) yarn in deep pink (D); 50g/88m/96yd

Magnetic closure

Lining and wadding/batting: 26 x 40cm (10¼ x 15¾in)

Lining for pocket: 15 x 27cm (6 x 10½in)

Interfacing for pocket: 12 x 12cm (4¾ x 4¾in)

TENSION (GAUGE)

10 sts x 16 rows over 10 x 10cm (4 x 4in) in st st

FINISHED SIZE

24 x 18cm (9½ x 7in) excluding handles

HANDLE (MAKE 2)

Using yarn B, cast on 4 sts.

Row 1: (k1, p1) twice.

This row forms moss st.

Continue in moss st until handle measures 40cm (15¾in).

Cast off.

MAKING UP

Using the photograph as a guide, thread a tapestry needle with yarn D and embroider crosses in chain stitch over the pattern (see page 111). The middle cross should join with the two outer ones to form two diamond shapes in the centre.

Press the bag pieces under a damp cloth (see page 115). Pin the bottom of the bag right sides together and sew the seam using backstitch (see page 116). Then sew the side seams using mattress stitch (see page 117). Pin and sew the handles to the inside top of the bag.

Follow the lining instructions on page 122 to fit the lining, and the instructions on page 121 to fit the magnetic closure.

Chart for intarsia Argyle pattern

Colour key:

⬜ (white)	Yarn A
🟦 (grey)	Yarn B
⬤	MB Yarn C

NB: Yarn D is used for embroidery only.

Techniques

TENSION (GAUGE)

It is important to do a tension (gauge) swatch before starting a project to ensure that you achieve the correct measurements used in the pattern. To measure a swatch, first knit a swatch in the stitch mentioned in the tension (gauge) part of the pattern (often in stocking stitch/US stockinette stitch). Knit a swatch a few stitches and rows bigger than the 10 x 10 cm (4 x 4in) tension (gauge) measurement.

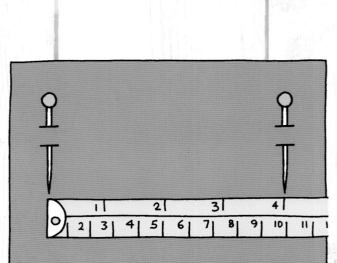

1 To measure stitches, place a tape measure horizontally across 10cm (4in) of your swatch, and place a pin vertically at the beginning and end of the 10cm (4in). Count the stitches between the two pins to the nearest stitch.

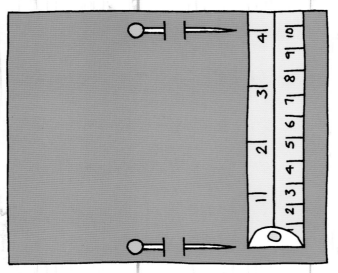

2 To measure rows, do the same but place the tape measure vertically with the pins horizontally and measure the number of rows in 10cm (4in).

If your tension (gauge) is not coming out correctly, adjust the needle size and knit another swatch. If there are too few stitches and rows, go down a needle size, and if there are too many go up a size.

COLOURWORK

Using Fair Isle

This is used for small areas of colour knitting with just a few stitches between colour changes. It is important to keep the tension (gauge) even when knitting Fair Isle, and not pull the strands at the back of the work too tightly.

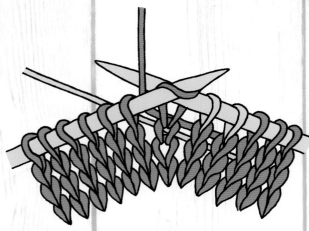

1 On RS rows, knit to the point of changing colour. Drop the first colour at the back of the work, and pick up the second colour. Strand the first colour loosely across the back until needed again.

2 On WS rows, work in the same way, but the strands will now be at the front of the work.

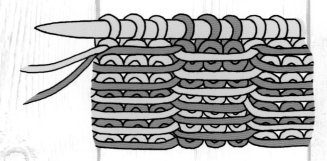

3 The back of the work should look neat with the strands not too loose or too tight.

Using intarsia

This is used when large areas of colour are knitted and you do not want long strands of yarn at the back of the work. Each square on the chart represents a stitch. Photocopy the chart and cross each row off with a pencil when it is done. Charts are normally read from right to left on RS rows and from left to right on WS rows.

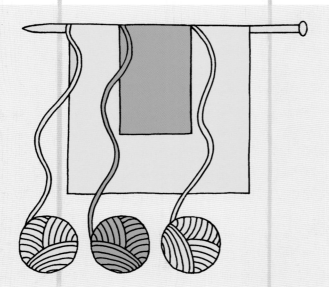

Before starting the pattern, wind off each colour to be knitted into small balls or onto bobbins, depending on how many you need in a row. The illustration shows a two-colour pattern with three areas of colour across the row being worked, so three separate balls of yarn, or bobbins, are needed.

When you get to the point where the colour is changed, twist the two strands of yarn around each other to prevent a hole forming.

When the intarsia is finished, tie the yarn securely at the back where the colour changes, and weave in the loose ends.

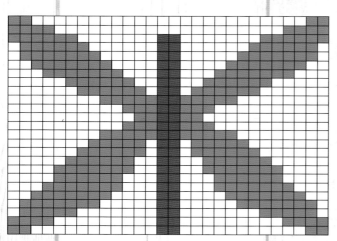

EMBELLISHMENTS

Appliqué

Appliqué is used to attach separately knitted or fabric pieces to the main piece of work. It can be combined with other embellishments such as embroidery, beads or sequins. The projects which use appliqué are Flowers & Beads and Bohemian.

1 Pin the appliqué piece to the main piece of knitting.

2 Sew on using a running stitch, in the yarn used for the appliqué piece and a tapestry needle.

Embroidery stitches

Embroidery is used to add an embellishment to a knitted piece. It is easier to do before it is sewn up so that you can easily access the back of the work. Chose one of the yarns used in the project in a contrasting colour, or a smooth version of a textured yarn. Use a large-eyed blunt tapestry needle, which is also used to sew up the pieces.

Running stitch

This is the simplest of stitches. Secure the yarn at the back of the work. Bring the yarn to the front, and insert the needle again to the back. Repeat, making a row of evenly sized long stitches on the front of the work.

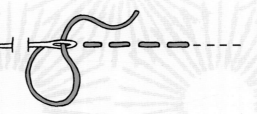

Blanket stitch

Blanket stitch is used as an edging embroidery stitch, often in a contrasting colour. It is also a useful way of neatening edges. The edge has a continuous line of stitching, with long stitches pointing in from the edge. The Folk bag uses blanket stitch around the edges including the pocket top, in a contrasting colour (see right).

1 To start, secure yarn at back of work. Bring the needle out at point 1, in at point 2 and out at 3, wrapping the yarn around the needle as shown.

2 Continue this across the edge, fastening off at the back when completed.

French knots

This stitch forms a small knot on the knitted piece. It is a good stitch to use for flower centres, and is used for berries in Autumn (see right).

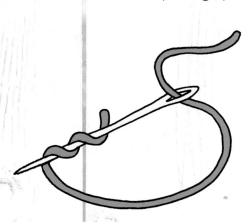

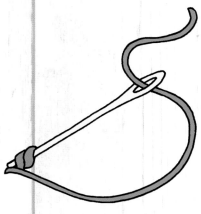

1 Secure the yarn at the back of the knitted piece. Bring the needle to the front, and wrap the yarn around the needle a few times depending on the size of the knot.

2 Insert the needle back into the work, keeping the yarn wrapped around the the needle securely, and pull the yarn through the twists and to the back of the work. Secure at the back.

Three finished French knots.

Chain stitch

Chain stitch is a frequently used embroidery stitch. It is useful to form a line with a bit more interest than a running stitch. It is used on several bags, including the Argyle bag (see right).

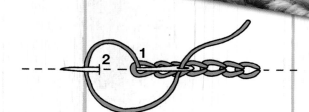

Secure the yarn at the back of the work. To start, bring the yarn out at point 1, make a loop, and re-insert the needle at point 1. Bring it out at point 2. Continue this to form a chain.

Lazy daisy stitch

This stitch is formed of individual chain stitches secured by a small stitch. It is a good stitch for making flowers, often used with a French knot at the centre, as on the Folk bag (see right).

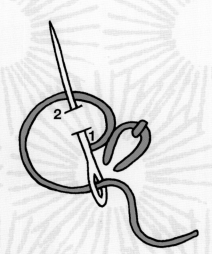

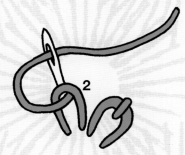

1 To start, secure the yarn at the back of the work. Bring the needle out at point 1, then reinsert the needle at point 1, bringing it out at point 2. Wrap the yarn around the needle as shown.

2 Insert the needle just above point 2, securing the chain stitch already made. Continue until 5 petals are completed.

3 This shows the completed flower. Secure the yarn at the back of the work.

Attaching beads and sequins

Beads and sequins are used to add interest and texture to knitted pieces. They can either be worked in while knitted, or sewn on afterwards. The ones used in these projects are sewn on after the knitted piece is completed. Use a sewing thread the same colour as the knitted piece, and a fine sewing needle to attach the beads and sequins.

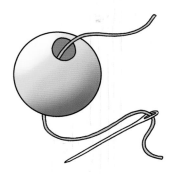

1 Decide where you want the bead to be placed. Secure the sewing thread at the back of the work. Bring the needle through the hole in the bead to the front, around the bead and back into the reverse of the work under the base of the bead.

2 Repeat this until the bead is secure, fastening off at the back.

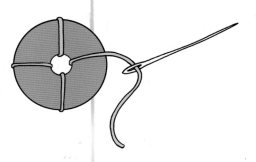

1 Decide where you want the sequin to be placed. Secure the sewing thread at the back of the work, and bring the needle up through the hole to the front. Take the thread across the sequin and into the back of the work again.

2 Repeat at least once more on the opposite side (see below) to secure the sequin. If preferred, you can repeat step 1 three times (see diagram above) for extra strength, before fastening off at the back.

Attaching knitted flowers

Knitted flowers are a good way to add an accent to a knitted project, and there are many different versions of flowers that can be made. The projects in the book which use knitted flowers are Daisy Basket, Flower Basket, Beach Bag, Roses and Flowers & Beads (see right). When knitting your flower, leave a long thread that can be used to attach it to the knitted piece.

1 Decide where you would like to place the flower. With a tapestry needle, thread the long tail end of yarn through it, and bring the needle point up through the centre of the flower.

2 Take the needle to the back, and repeat until the flower is secure. Finish off at the back.

How to make pompoms

Pompoms are a traditional embellishment that add interest to a project and are fun to make. Two of the bags, Two-Tone and Nordic, have pompoms added to the ties. You can buy plastic pompom makers which come in various sizes and can be re-used. The original method used here with cardboard pieces is just as good, and you can decide on the size of the pompom.

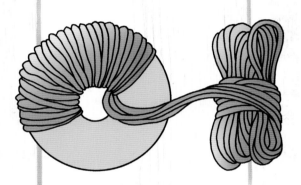

1 Cut two circles of card slightly larger than you want the pompom to be. Cut two smaller holes at the centre. Place these pieces of card together. Wind some yarn into a little ball that will fit through the hole at the centre. Wind the yarn through the hole as shown, until there is only a small gap left. You can use a tapestry needle for the last part.

2 Insert the point of some sharp scissors into the gap between the circles and cut through the yarn.

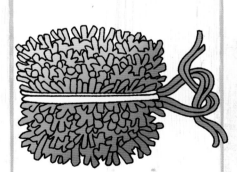

3 Wind some doubled yarn between the gaps in the card, and tie securely a few times. Cut through the card and gently pull away from the pompom. Trim the pompom to shape. Use the long piece of yarn to attach the pompom to the project.

The finished pompom

MAKING UP

Blocking

Blocking is a way of pressing the knitted pieces to the correct size and shape before sewing up. It also makes the edges flat and easier to sew up.

Pure wool yarns can be pressed under a damp cloth. Cottons and mixes can be pressed under a dry cloth. Do not put the iron directly onto any knitting. If there is a deep texture such as a cable, only press the edges where you will be sewing up a seam. If you try to press the cable itself, you will flatten the design.

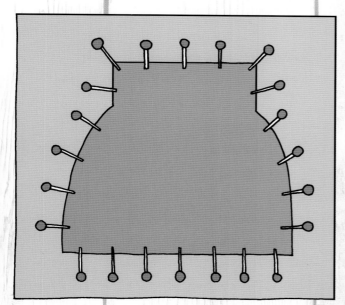

1 Place the knitted piece onto an ironing board or flat surface, on a few layers of towels. Measure the piece and pin it to the correct size stated in the pattern.

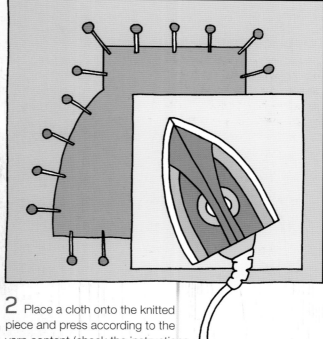

2 Place a cloth onto the knitted piece and press according to the yarn content (check the instructions on the ballband).

3 Leave the knitted piece to cool and dry completely before unpinning it.

Weaving in loose ends

You will need to weave in the loose ends of the knitted pieces before sewing up and afterwards. Before sewing up, use a tapestry needle to weave in any loose ends of yarn on the back of the work. This is for when there has been a new ball of yarn added, or where there is a colour change.

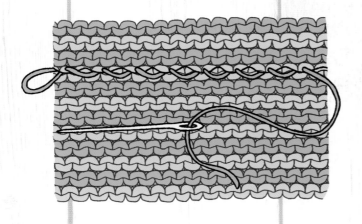

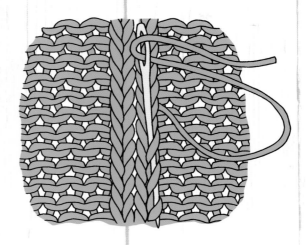

Colour change

At the end of a ball of yarn, or where you have a colour change, for example with stripes (see above), take the yarn along the row for a few stitches in the back loops of the WS of the work. Pull securely and snip off the end.

Weaving into a seam

After the bags are sewn up, weave in the ends of yarn on the seams on the WS of the work. Take the yarn ends along a small part of the seam, as shown above, then snip off the end.

Backstitch

Backstitch can be used on any seam, and forms a neat firm seam. On all the bags it is used on the bottom seam.

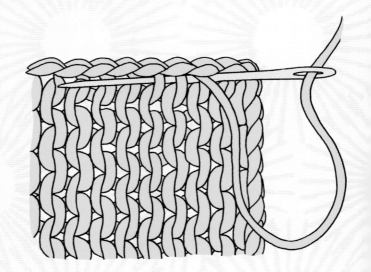

1 Place the pieces RS together. Pin in place.

2 Sew the seam using backstitch.

Mattress stitch

This is the best way of sewing up any vertical seams, and is almost invisible. The illustration shows joining stocking stitch (US stockinette stitch). For reverse stocking stitch and any other stitch, follow the instructions but sew into the first whole stitch you can nearest the edge. Use the same yarn as the knitted pieces to join them together and a blunt-ended tapestry needle.

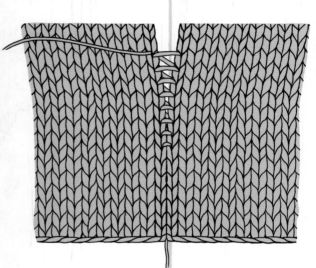

1 Line up the two pieces to be sewn together so that they are level, with right sides facing upwards.

2 Working from the front, insert the needle into the centre of one stitch on one side of the knitting, then repeat for the opposite side. Move up the seam, picking up a stitch every row until the seam is completed. Leave the stitches loose for a few rows, then pull gently together. The gap will disappear to form a neat seam.

FASTENINGS

Zips

Zips are a useful way of having a continuous fastening with no gaps. They can be used on a variety of knitted projects. They are used for the make-up bag that accompanies the Two-Tone bag (see below and page 32), and the purse to match the Folk bag (see right and page 36).

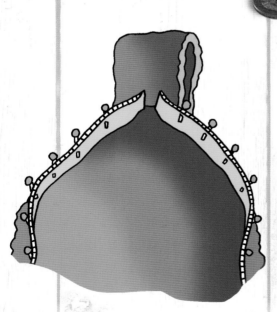

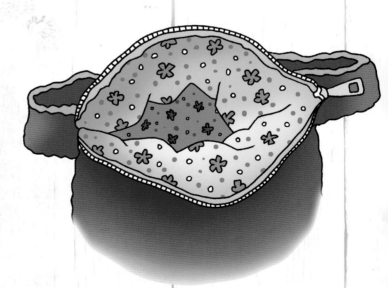

1 With the zip open, pin both sides to the top of the inside of the knitted bag, with the teeth at the top. Sew in place by hand with sewing thread in a running stitch below the teeth so that the zip can be opened easily, and leave a space for the lining to be sewn on so that the stitching doesn't show.

2 Prepare the lining as decribed on page 122, then pin it in place just below the teeth so that the zip can be opened easily. Sew in place using running stitch, or a small slip stitch if you prefer.

Buttons

Buttons can be both practical – used with a buttonhole – and decorative. The ones in this book are used as a decorative feature, with the closures being made with a snap fastening. Choose one that suits the project with the size in proportion to the tab it is placed on. To sew on the button, choose a sewing thread close to the colour of the knitted piece, and use a fine sewing needle. Doubling up the thread will make sewing on quicker and more secure.

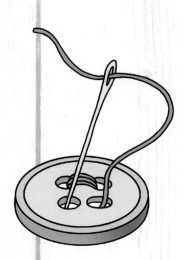

1 Decide where you would like the button to be placed. Secure the sewing thread at the back of the work, then bring the needle up through one of the holes to the front. Thread the needle back through the opposite hole to the back.

2 If the button has two pairs of holes, bring the needle up through one of these holes, then back down to the reverse through its opposite hole (see above). Repeat several times, then do the same with the other pair of holes. Fasten off at the back.

Snap fasteners

Snap fasteners are a practical way to fasten pieces together and easy to open and close. Choose a sewing thread close to the colour of the knitted pieces, and use a fine sewing needle. Doubling up the thread will make sewing on quicker and more secure.

1 Snap fasteners come in two sections: a ball and socket (see above). The ball at the centre of one section presses or snaps tightly into the socket at the centre of the other.

2 Decide where the snap fastener is to be placed. Secure the thread at the back of the work. Bring the needle up through one of the holes, around the edge and into the back. Repeat this a few times for each hole until the snap fastener is secure (see above).

3 For the second half of the fastener, position it to line up with the first half and repeat step 2.

Magnetic closures

Magnetic closures are a useful way to fasten pieces together. They are neat, do not show from the outside and do not need sewing on. They consist of two magnetic ball and socket pieces, and a flat metal washer for each piece (see right).

For the bags that use these closures, they are placed centrally, just below the top of the lining, before the lining is sewn in place.

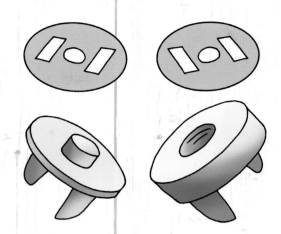

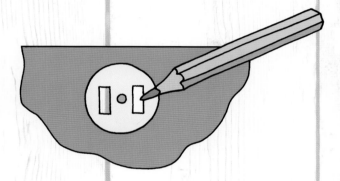

1 Decide where you want the closure to go. Place the washer where you want the first side of the closure to go, and mark the inside of the holes on the lining with a pencil.

2 Make a small cut with sharp scissors or a seam ripper in the lining where the marks are. These will be the position for the prongs.

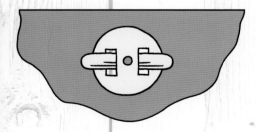

3 Place one of the closures onto the holes and push the prongs through the holes, from the front to the back of the lining, placing the washer over the prongs at the back. Bend the prongs outwards.

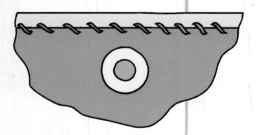

4 Repeat with the second half of the closure, on the opposite side from the first half. Then sew the lining in place as directed in the making up instructions.

LINING

Lining is used to neaten the inside of the bags so that you do not see the back of the knitting. It also adds another layer, and gives the inside of the bags a splash of colour and print. Choose your own lining fabrics to personalise your bag.

Wadding/batting

Wadding/batting is used to give some bulk to the knitted pieces. It is also used for projects such as quilt-making. Along with the lining, it adds some firmness to the knitted bags. Wadding/batting can be bought in various weights, but here I have used a mid-weight type that is 135g (4oz) per square metre.

Interfacing

Interfacing is used on knitted bags where wadding/batting would be too bulky, to give the knitted and lining pieces a bit more firmness. It is also used on all the inside pockets, along with lining. The iron-on kind is the easiest to use.

Lining the bags

Below are the general instructions for all bags, with the exception of Folk (page 36), Nautical (page 52), Bohemian (page 56) and Grapes & Bobbles (page 72), the instructions for which appear on their respective pages. For the measurements for each bag's lining, wadding/batting and interfacing, see the information in individual patterns.

The instructions below are for bags with wadding/batting. For the bags shown opposite, simply follow these instructions, using interfacing instead of wadding/batting for both the lining and the pocket.

1 Cut out the lining fabric and wadding/batting for the main bag, and lining fabric and interfacing for the pocket according to measurements given in each pattern (NB: if the print on the lining does not have a specific direction, cut in one piece and fold it at the centre. If it does, cut it in two pieces and sew them together with the seam at the bottom, keeping the print on the pocket going in the same direction as the lining).

2 Pin the wadding/batting to the lining if it is being used. Fold over to the WS a 1.5cm (⅝in) seam allowance at the top of one side of the bag and machine stitch in place.

3 Fold the lining fabric for the pocket right sides together and press. It is neater to have the folded edge at the top of the pocket. If using iron-on interfacing, press this on now, with one edge against the fold. Sew one side and the top. Clip corner, turn pocket right side out and press again. Pin and sew the remaining seam.

4 Pin the seam allowance on the open side. Pin and sew the pocket in place around the sides and bottom, a little below the top at the centre.

5 Fit the magnetic closure (see page 121) now if you are adding one.

6 Pin the lining pieces together around the sides and bottom and try inside the bag for fit, pinning around the top to check. Make sure that it fits well and adjust if needed (it is better for the lining to be slightly smaller than the bag in depth and width to avoid it looking loose).

7 Once the fit is adjusted, sew the side and bottom seams, RS facing.

8 Place the lining inside the bag, referring to the making up instructions, and pin to the knitted piece, then hand sew it in place.

Bags that use interfacing instead of wadding/batting:

Leaves, page 40

Waves & Pods, page 60

Lacy Lattice, page 76

Butterfly, page 80

Lace & Ribbon, page 84

Braided cords

Braided cords can be made from the yarns used to make the bag, or from any yarn or material that works with the design. Textured Circles (page 24) uses a thin faux suede cord that is braided, Folk (page 36) uses pieces of braided fabric, and Beach Bag (page 44) has long knitted strips braided together.

1 To make a braided cord, first cut some lengths of yarn to the measurements stated on the pattern. Tie these together at one end. Put this end under something heavy, or pin it to something solid.

2 Make a braid in the usual way. At the end, tie another knot a little bit before the end. Trim the ends so that they are even.

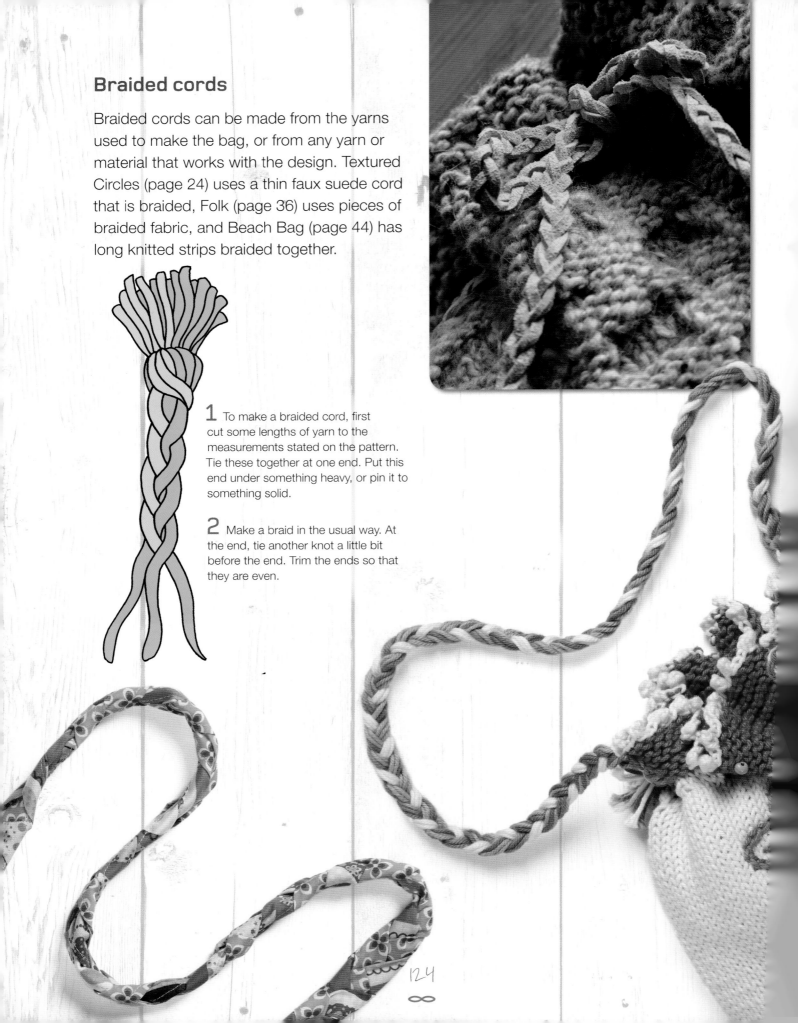

Bag handles

There are many different
types of bag handles. Knitted
handles can be made in a variety
of yarns, stitches and lengths. There is
an excellent choice available for bought
handles, both online and in craft shops.
These come in different materials such
as plastic, leather, faux leather, bamboo
and smooth wood.

There are many different shapes, and the
way they are attached will depend on the
type of handles used. These are different
for each bag and are described in
the patterns in the making
up section.

ABBREVIATIONS

The list below gives the most commonly used abbreviations in this book.

CDI	central double increase: (k1tbl, k1) in next st, insert left-hand needle point behind vertical strand running downward between the 2 sts just made and k1tbl into it to make third st
cm	centimetre(s)
cn	cable needle
cont	continue
C6B	slip next 3 sts on to cn, hold sts to back of work, k3, k3 from cn
C6F	slip next 3 sts on to cn, hold sts to front of work, k3, k3 from cn
dec	decrease(ing)
g st	garter stitch
in	inch(es)
k	knit
kfb	knit into front and back of next st
kfbf	k into front, back and front again of next st
k2tog	knit 2 stitches together
k3tog	knit 3 stitches together
LH	left hand
m1	make one stitch; pick up horizontal strand of yarn between st just worked and next st and knit it
m1p	make st by picking up and purling into back of strand before next st
MB	make bobble; k into front, back and front of next st, turn, p3, turn, k3, turn, p3, turn, sl 1, k2tog, psso
p	purl

p2tog	purl two stitches together
psso	pass slipped st over
rep	repeat
rev st st	reverse stocking (stockinette) stitch
RH	right hand
RS	right side
ssk	sl next 2 sts singly to RH needle knitwise, insert tip of LH needle through front loop of both sts and k2tog
st(s)	stitch(es)
sl	slip
sl1	slip 1 st
tbl	through back loop
TW3B	twist 3 back: sl next st onto a cn and hold at back of work, k next 2 sts from LH needle, then p st from cn
Tw4B	twist 4 back: slip next st on to cn, hold st to back of work, k3, p1 from cn
Tw5B	twist 5 back: slip next 2 sts on to cn, hold sts to back of work, k3, p2 from cn
Tw3F	twist 3 front: sl next 2 sts on to cn and hold at front of work, p next st from LH needle, then k sts from cn
Tw4F	twist 4 front: slip next 3 sts on to cn, hold sts to front of work, p1, k3 from cn
Tw5F	twist 5 front: slip next 3 sts on to cn, hold sts to front of work, p2, k3 from cn
WS	wrong side
yo	yarn over needle
yf	yarn forward
yfrn	yarn forward and around needle
yd	yard(s)

Yarn conversions

UK	US	Australia
4-ply	fingering	4-ply
DK or 8-ply	DK or light worsted	8-ply
aran	worsted	10-ply

Simple Bags

Flowers & Beads

1 Rowan British Sheep Breeds Chunky Undyed, colour: Blue Faced Leicester, chunky (bulky); 100% wool. Ball weight: 100g/110m/120yd.

2 Rowan Fur (eyelash yarn),colour: Polar, chunky (bulky); 97% wool, 3% polyamide. Ball weight: 50g/60m/66yd.

3 Debbie Bliss Cashmerino Aran, colours: Mauve, Lime, aran (10-ply/worsted); 55% wool, 33% acrylic, 12% cashmere. Ball weight: 50g/90m/98yd.

Flower Basket

1 Debbie Bliss Cashmerino Aran, colour: Mauve, aran (10-ply/worsted); 55% wool, 33% acrylic, 12% cashmere. Ball weight: 50g/90m/98yd.

2 Debbie Bliss Angel, colour: Lilac, 1–3-ply (lace weight); 76% mohair, 24% silk. Ball weight: 25g/200m/218yd.

Textured Circles

Debbie Bliss Luxury Tweed Aran, colour: Silver, aran (10-ply/worsted); 90% wool, 10% angora. Ball weight: 50g/88m/96yd.

Roses

Noro Silk Garden, colour: 389, aran (10-ply/worsted); 45% mohair, 45% silk, 10% wool. Ball weight: 50g/100m/109yd.

Two-Tone

1 Rowan Creative Focus Worsted, colour: Natural, aran (10-ply/worsted); 75% wool, 25% alpaca. Ball weight: 100g/200–220m/219–240yd.

2 Rowan Felted Tweed Aran, colour: Madras, aran (10-ply/worsted); 50% merino, 25% alpaca, 25% viscose. Ball weight: 50g/87m/95yd.

Folk

1 Drops Alaska, colours: Dark Red, Off White, aran (10-ply/worsted); 100% wool. Ball weight: 50g/70m/76yd.

2 Drops Nepal, colours: Light Olive, Light Grey Green, Cerise, Orange, Goldenrod, aran (10-ply/worsted); 65% wool, 35% alpaca. Ball weight: 50g/75m/82yd.

Leaves

Rowan Big Wool, colour: Deer, super chunky (super bulky); 100% merino wool. Ball weight: 100g/80m/87yd.

Summer Bags

Beach Bag

Rico Essentials Cotton Aran, colours: Natural, Turquoise, Light Pistachio, Violet, Candy Pink, aran (10-ply/worsted); 100% cotton. Ball weight: 50g/85m/93yd.

Daisy Basket

Rowan Handknit Cotton, colours: Linen, Bleached, Bee, DK (8-ply/light worsted); 100% cotton. Ball weight: 50g/85m/93yd.

Nautical

Rico Essentials Cotton Aran, colours: Natural, Dark Blue, Cherry, aran (10-ply/worsted); 100% cotton. Ball weight: 50g/85m/93yd.

Bohemian

Rowan Handknit Cotton, colours: Ecru, Sugar, Florence, Ochre, Gooseberry, DK (8-ply/light worsted); 100% cotton. Ball weight: 50g/85m/93yd.

Cablework

Waves & Pods

Mirasol Sulka, colour: Ash, chunky (bulky); 60% merino wool, 20% alpaca, 20% silk. Ball weight: 50g/50m/55yd.

Bobbles & Waves

Sublime Luxurious Tweed DK, colour: Bluff Blue, DK (8-ply/light worsted); 60% wool, 40% cotton. Ball weight: 50g/135m/147yd.

Rope Cable

Rowan Felted Tweed Aran, colour: Pebble, aran (10-ply/worsted); 50% merino wool, 25% alpaca, 25% viscose. Ball weight: 50g/87m/95yd.

Grapes & Bobbles

Artesano Aran, colour: Pine, aran (10-ply/worsted); 50% wool, 50% alpaca. Skein weight: 100g/132m/144yd.

Evening

Lacy Lattice

1 Debbie Bliss Luxury Silk DK, colour: Silver, DK (8-ply/light worsted); 100% silk. Ball weight: 50g/100m/109yd.

2 Debbie Bliss Angel, colour: Silver, 1–3-ply (lace weight); 76% mohair, 24% silk. Ball weight: 25g/200m/218yd.

Butterfly

Rico Essentials Cotton DK, colours: Silver, Teal, Fuchsia, DK (8-ply/light worsted); 100% cotton. Ball weight: 50g/115m/125yd.

Lace & Ribbon

Sirdar Soukie, colour; Dusky Rose, DK (8-ply/light worsted); 40% polyester, 33% acrylic, 27% cotton. Ball weight: 50g/110m/120yd.

Colourwork

Nordic

1 Drops Alaska, colours: Off White, Dark Turquoise, Dark Red, Purple Mix, aran (10-ply/worsted); 100% wool. Ball weight: 50g/70m/76yd.

2 Drops Nepal, colours: Light Grey Green, Light Olive, aran (10-ply/worsted); 65% wool, 35% alpaca. Ball weight: 50g/75m/82yd.

Flower Fair Isle & Rib

1 Rowan Felted Tweed Aran, colour: Madras, aran (10-ply/worsted); 50% merino wool, 25% alpaca, 25% viscose. Ball weight: 50g/87m/95yd.

2 Rowan Felted Tweed, colours: Avocado, Rage, Bilberry, DK (8-ply/light worsted); 50% merino wool; 25% alpaca, 25% viscose. Ball weight: 50g/175m/191yd.

Autumn

1 Rowan Felted Tweed Aran, colours: Pebble, Dark Violet, Glade, Plum, aran (10-ply/worsted); 50% merino wool, 25% alpaca, 25% viscose. Ball weight: 50g/87m/95yd.

2 Debbie Bliss Luxury Tweed Aran, colour: Fuchsia, aran (10-ply/worsted); 50% merino wool, 25% alpaca, 25% viscose. Ball weight: 50g/88m/96yd.

Argyle

1 Rowan Big Wool, colours; Linen, Burnt Orange, super chunky (super bulky); 100% merino wool. Ball weight: 100g/80m/87yd.

2 Rowan Felted Tweed Aran, colour: Plum, aran (10-ply/worsted); 50% merino wool, 25% alpaca, 25% viscose. Ball weight: 50g/87m/95yd.

3 Debbie Bliss Luxury Tweed Aran, colour: Fuchsia, aran (10-ply/worsted); 90% wool, 10% angora. Ball weight: 50g/88m/96yd.

INDEX